DEAR FRIEND

Part two of *The Healing Journey* offers words of comfort and strength from one who knows what it's like to be gravely ill—and then to experience the miraculous. It is built around a series of remarkable letters Reid Henson wrote to other cancer patients, tracing the spiritual growth that resulted in his "miracle." These letters offer an intense look at a patient's innermost thoughts and feelings. Originally mailed once a week, they form an ongoing meditation on such topics as becoming a "student of life," dealing with guilt and self-blame, conquering fear, and becoming more aware of God's will.

"Once I invited the spiritual aspect of me into the problem, I found that Spirit can transform the human mind. It was only then that I realized I did not have to figure out all aspects of my illness in order to get well."

THE *Healing Journey*

BY

O. CARL SIMONTON, M.D.,
AND

REID M. HENSON
WITH

BRENDA HAMPTON

BANTAM BOOKS
NEW YORK · TORONTO · LONDON · SYDNEY · AUCKLAND

THE HEALING JOURNEY
A Bantam Book
PUBLISHING HISTORY
Bantam hardcover edition published May 1992
Bantam paperback edition/March 1994

ISBN 0-553-56578-8

Published simultaneously in the United States and Canada

Bantam Books are published by Bantam Books, a division of Bantam Doubleday Dell
Publishing Group, Inc. Its trademark, consisting of the words "Bantam Books" and the
portrayal of a rooster, is Registered in U.S. Patent and Trademark Office and in other
countries. Marca Registrada. Bantam Books, 1540 Broadway, New York, New York
10036.

PRINTED IN THE UNITED STATES OF AMERICA
OPM   0 9 8 7 6 5 4 3 2

Contents

PART II

THE LETTERS OF REID HENSON

"I believe they come for the healing, for in hearing the troubles and longings and truths of other lives no matter how . . . frail or perfect . . . they see the common thread, that it isn't about women and men and young and old and black and white and rich and poor and famous and unknown, it's about this deep and abiding and relentless yearning for a healing to take place in all of us and between all of us. . . ."

—MICHAEL LALLY
The Healing Poem

Introduction

With this book, I invite you to begin your journey to health. I ask you to consider that you can only begin this journey from where you are in your life experience, not from where you want to be, and I realize that for many of you this journey begins with the diagnosis of cancer or some other life-threatening disease.

While this is a very difficult place to begin, it is also a very powerful position, because you now have a compelling reason to learn whatever you need to know to change the course of your disease and your life. And while the road ahead will be difficult, I want to assure you that this can also be a joyous journey, a joyful process. It involves work and responsibility, but, above all, it's about discovering what in life excites and motivates you, and how you can use that to come into harmony with the world around you— and return to health.

When I co-authored *Getting Well Again* in 1978, I knew that the techniques I used worked, and since then medical science has shown much more of how and why. Over the past decade, I have continued to refine and expand my techniques, finding that the most powerful approach to cancer is one that involves physical, mental, and spiritual processes that systematically identify the issues around illness and methodically bring about changes that lead to health.

Since that first book, I have learned a lot more about healing, and I have met some remarkable patients. I am going to introduce you to one of those patients, Reid Henson. We are going to follow Reid's journey from a terminal diagnosis to health, allowing you to take an indepth look at one person, to see how the program worked for him, and to show you how you can use his creative approach to the program as a stimulus for your own way of doing this work.

In addition, I am going to give you alternative approaches and techniques, as well as show you how to set up a program for health that is unique to your situation.

I have been working with a physical/mental/spiritual approach to cancer since 1971. I have treated thousands of patients, and my patients have a relatively high rate of recovery, even from so-called "terminal" illnesses. I know that each patient has his or her own struggles in life, but I also know that facing whatever issues life presents makes a difference in getting well.

Using this book, you have access to the Simonton Cancer Center's program, and with that, the opportunity to participate in the improvement of your own health. If you use the book as it is intended to be used, you will probably find something to do about your health every day for at least the next year. And for those of you who might feel alone in your work or disconnected from others because of your illness, I think you will find great comfort and strength in getting to know Reid Henson through his series of letters to you. He's been there. He knows what it feels like to deal with cancer over many years, as well as what it's like to be well again.

I hope you'll think of us as a doctor/patient team, extending our help to you in love and understanding, and with great hope for your recovery.

—O. Carl Simonton, M.D.

PART **I**

THE
SIMONTON CENTER
PROGRAM

1

Body, Mind, and Spirit

How We Combat Cancer and Other
Serious Diseases

Cancer patients triggered my interest in the connection between the body and the mind—not physicians or psychologists, but cancer patients. My interest in this field was aroused during the first year of my residency, when I found that I couldn't get patients with advanced cancer to comply with treatment in a positive way. They saw no reason to involve themselves, because they had no confidence in their ability to get well. They felt hopeless.

Prior to this experience, during my internship, I had made several widely recognized discoveries in basic cell biology and radiation biology, so I very much believed I was going to be part of the team or teams involved in finding and implementing a cure for cancer. I was determined to be one of the leading radiation oncologists in the country. I had been selected "intern of the year" during my internship, and I was returning to the University of Oregon Medical School to a prized residency. It was a very high time in my life.

I was fully confident that I could contribute to a cure for cancer, but until my residency, I had not considered that a patient might have something to do with whether or not a treatment worked. I was amazed that many of my patients didn't seem motivated to get better. They not only had no confidence in their own ability to get well, they had no confidence in me or any other doctor treating them for cancer. So I began to look at this problem and to explore the possibility of getting patients to involve themselves willingly, believing that this would increase the effectiveness of their treatments.

In my search for ways to mobilize my patients' inner resources, I studied meditation, visualization, positive thinking, Eastern philosophies, shamans, fire-walking, Silva Mind Control, and many, many other approaches, incorporating what I learned into my work. With my colleagues at the Cancer Counseling and Research Center in Fort Worth, I developed many methods that brought about dramatic changes in my patients' attitudes—and in their response to medical treatment. From 1974 to 1981, we conducted a seven-year outcome study of our patients and found their term of survival to be twice as long as the survival times reported from other leading cancer centers, and more than three times as long as the national averages for survival of people with similar advanced cancers. I first reported on this work to the World Cancer Conference in Buenos Aires in 1978, and subsequently published *Getting Well Again*, through which our methods became available to the general public.

THE SCIENTIFIC EVIDENCE FOR OUR APPROACH

The final results of our seven-year study were reported to other professionals at the annual meeting of the Australian

Medical Association in February 1981. My research team and I had investigated the survival rates of people with advanced lung cancer, advanced cancer of the bowel, and advanced breast cancer. In all three categories, the survival times we observed were approximately twice as long as those observed at the leading cancer centers throughout the world.

One of the strongest points of our study was the follow-up. We were able to maintain follow-up reports on 98 percent of our patients, despite the fact that they came from all parts of the United States and many foreign countries. The weakest aspect of the study was that we could afford to do it only on our own patient population, a selected group, without the randomization and a matched control population, necessary for maximum scientific credibility. This would have been the next step, but limited funding prevented us from continuing.

However, such a study has now been completed and was published in October 1989. The research, done at Stanford University and the University of California at Berkeley, represents the highest standard in scientific evidence—in a controlled, randomized study. The researchers studied women with advanced breast cancer, and the results, which were reported by Dr. David Spiegel of Stanford, are very exciting. In their controlled study, they followed fifty women in the counseled group. In our selected population, we had seventy-one women. Their median survival time was 36.6 months in the counseled group, ours was 38.5 months. The survival of their control group—women who were not counseled—was 18.9 months; our calculated historical control population survival, based on figures from other centers, was 18.0 months.

These results are especially gratifying because, as Dr. Spiegel has freely admitted, the researchers had set out to disprove claims that counseling could affect survival! Instead, working with admirable objectivity, they have strengthened our conclusions with the highest order of clinical research.

Some of our patients at the Simonton Cancer Center are very interested in such research, and in the pages that follow, I'd like to outline more of the evidence for a mind/body approach. Other patients, however, intuitively feel that this approach is right for them, and want to get on with the work directly. If this is the case for you, feel free to skip to page 13, "New Findings, New Conclusions."

While scientific proof of the mind–body connection still makes headlines, doctors working with individual patients have observed such a connection since the beginning of recorded medical history. The first statement regarding the relationship between emotions and cancer that I know of was written in 140 A.D. by the ancient Greek physician Galen, who observed and recorded the relationship between depression and breast cancer. Even earlier, in the writings of Plato, Socrates refers several times to the importance of addressing the mind and emotions in illness. Socrates claimed that to ignore this relationship was to be less than a complete physician.

This clinical wisdom persisted into the early twentieth century. Lawrence LeShan, whom I consider to be one of the primary authorities on the history of psychological aspects of cancer, did an extensive review of standard medical textbooks written between 1800 and 1900. In his recent book *Cancer as a Turning Point*, LeShan states that all but one of the nineteen books he studied contained a statement similar to the following: "Of course, the emotional life history [the books used a lot of different phrases for this, but the meaning was the same] plays a major role in the tendency of the person to get cancer and in the progress of the cancer."

Meanwhile, however, medicine was going in the opposite direction. In their long struggle to put medicine on a scientific basis, doctors had come to reject the role of mind and spirit in health, relegating it to the "mysticism" of the past. And the "scientific" approach, regarding the body as a machine that can be repaired like a machine, did bring about spectacular advances in our understanding and treatment of disease. By the time I began my practice, this medical model dominated our culture, our training as physicians, and all our medical institutions. Patients came to us wanting their bodies to be "fixed," and we were eager to fix them.

A new turning point came in the 1960s, when the prestigious New York Academy of Sciences sponsored two conferences, both entitled "The Psychophysiological Aspects of Cancer." These conferences brought together the leading researchers from all over the world. Some of the most important papers of the decade were presented at these two conferences and later published in the *Annals of the New York Academy of Sciences* (January 1966 and October 1969). Together they represent major works on both clinical observations and animal research that thoroughly discuss the interrelatedness of the mind, emotions, and cancer.

In 1973, C. B. Thomas of Johns Hopkins Medical School, reported on her study of psychological factors as predictors of five disease states. Published in the *Johns Hopkins Medical Journal,* this was one of the first prospective studies—i.e. one that studied the psychological characteristics of people *before* they were diagnosed. The disease that was most clearly correlated with psychological traits was cancer. Dr. Thomas's observations were based on thirty years of prospective data, and she concluded that the following characteristics predisposed a person to develop cancer:

- Responding to stress with a sense of hopelessness
- Bottling up emotions or having impaired emotional outlets
- Perceiving a lack of closeness with one or both parents

The health effects of hopelessness and bottling up emotions have now been reported by many clinicians. For example, Leonard Derogatis at Johns Hopkins and Stephen Greer at Kings College Hospital in London have focused on personality factors and psychological coping strategies as predictors of survival rates in women with breast cancer. Their conclusions are similar, in that the coping strategies are correlated with survival. The highest rate of survival has been associated with women who can be described as having a fighting spirit, and the lowest with those who feel hopeless. Dr. Greer is now doing research to see if coping strategies can be changed, and if, when they are changed, the survival rate changes also.

I believe that the answers are that the strategies *can* be changed, and that, if they are, the survival rate changes. In our own experience with our patients we see powerful evidence of this, although of course there are areas that need to be evaluated extensively by further research. There is so much still to discover, not only about the relationship between personality and disease, but about how to interact with and change the personality in order to decrease the incidence of disease, and to increase the healing prospects of those already ill.

In the study of psychological aspects of illness, I think the leading body of work by a single investigator is that of Ronald Grossarth-Maticek, the Yugoslav psychologist now working at the University of Heidelberg, Germany. He has recently collaborated with the world-renowned British psychologist Hans Eysenck. Maticek began studying disease-

prone personality types in the mid-1960s. He categ
cancer prone personalities as people with repressed e
tions and hopelessness, and heart disease personalities
people who primarily have issues around hostility and ag-
gression.

In one study, Maticek followed 1300 Yugoslavs for more
than ten years. Although they had not previously been
diagnosed, Maticek was able to predict their deaths from
cancer or heart disease with statistically significant accuracy. In another study, he divided people with disease-
prone personalities into two groups, half of which received
counseling and half of which did not. He found that he was
able to alter death rates from cancer and heart disease with
counseling. This work is exciting because for the first time,
we are seeing that it is possible to prevent cancer in people
who are psychologically predisposed to it by counseling
them. The counseling methods Maticek used included relaxation, desensitization, modeling, suggestion, hypnosis,
visualization, and other standard behavioral techniques.
(You will be learning some of these techniques in this
book.) Maticek later repeated these studies with Hans Eysenck. With as little as six hours of group therapy, he and
Eysenck found they could significantly alter death rates
from both cancer and heart disease.

In yet another study, Maticek and Eysenck followed
twenty-four cancer patients who completed a counseling
program and compared their progress to twenty-four
matched patients who did not receive counseling. They
found that the median survival time was five years for the
counseled group and three years for the non-counseled
group. This compares well with both our work and the work
reported in the Stanford/UC Berkely study.

The most amazing study to me is one that Maticek did
with one hundred women with "terminal" breast cancer.

who elected to have no chemotherapy for their advanced breast cancer were matched with fifty who elected to receive chemotherapy. The survival times were as follows:

- Those women who received no therapy at all had a median survival time of eleven months.
- Among those who received chemotherapy only the median survival time was fourteen months.
- Among those receiving counseling only, the median survival time was fifteen months.
- Among those receiving both chemotherapy and counseling, it was twenty-two months.

Keep in mind that these were women with advanced breast cancer, and that these are median survival times— meaning that while some women died earlier, others survived much longer.

Maticek's results confirm scientifically what many of us in the field have believed and acted on for years: The best treatment for cancer is to take the best that contemporary medicine has to offer, presented in a supportive way, together with the best that counseling has to offer. The results are better than for either chemotherapy or other medical treatments alone or for counseling alone.

The most recent support for this approach has come from Dean Ornish's study of people being treated for serious coronary heart disease, first reported in *Lancet* in July 1990, and also in his book *Reversing Heart Disease*. One group of patients was counseled to make lifestyle changes in the same areas we stress with our patients, including exercise, diet, relaxation, and work with support groups. A second group received only standard medical treatment. Dr. Ornish reported that 82 percent of the counseled group showed blockage reversal; blockage worsened in 53 percent of the control group.

Another important question about counseling concerns timing: At what point should psychological therapy be incorporated into a patient's program for health? Clinicians have long known that there are proper times to approach patients about dealing with emotional issues around illness. One of the leading researchers in this area is Kristina Brode of Germany.

According to Brode, patients who are experiencing the shock of being diagnosed with cancer or the shock of recurrent disease after a significant interval of remission often respond with defensive coping strategies, including denial. They may seem surprisingly calm or make plans to go on with life as usual, as if nothing had happened. These defensive coping strategies should be respected. In other words, following the initial diagnosis or the diagnosis of a recurrence, the patient may not be ready for counseling. In addition to solid reassurance and nurturing at this time, the patient may respond well to simple relaxation techniques and gentle massage. However, this may be an appropriate time for family members and other support people to do intensive work in counseling.

Brode's work shows that the shock around initial diagnosis frequently lasts from three to six months. Similar reactions to the diagnosis of recurrence generally last two to four weeks. One of the key statements that patients tend to make as they are coming out of this period of shock and become ready to take a more active role in the healing process is to ask, "What else can I do to get well?" If counseling is forced on a person with cancer before he or she is ready, the tendency is to move into hopelessness.

Brode's work shows the importance of honoring a patient's own sense of timing. For example, if you are reviewing this book before giving it to a sick family member or friend, be aware that he or she may not yet be ready for it. You might mention that you think it would be helpful, but then let that person ask for it or choose when to read it.

Before we leave the area of scientific evidence, I want to touch on another important and relatively new discipline known as psycho-neuro-immunology. Past research with patients has clearly demonstrated the mind–body connection, but hasn't explained how it works. Psycho-neuro-immunology is now providing some of the answers, helping us to understand better how the emotions are translated into chemical substances (information molecules) that impact the body's immune system and other healing mechanisms. Some of the most exciting work in this field has been done by Candace Pert, the former chief of brain biochemistry at the National Institute of Mental Health. She is the co-discoverer of the first neuropeptide receptor, one of the chemical message receivers that acts in the communication of emotion. Her discovery was made in 1973, and since then more than fifty neuropeptides have been identified.

We know now that there are at least three systems in the body that can communicate emotions at the physical level. One is the endocrine system, which communicates through the hormones; the second is the nervous system, which connects directly to white blood cells; and the third is the family of communication molecules, which includes neuropeptides, neurotransmitters, growth factors, and cytokines, which influence cellular activity as well as cell division mechanisms and genetic functioning.

Through new technological advances, scientists in the laboratory can see that certain nerve fibers actually end on the surface of certain white blood cells, physical evidence that white blood cells receive direct messages from the nervous system, messages that originate from the brain.

White blood cells are key components of the body's immune system, working to identify and eliminate foreign material such as bacteria and cancer cells. So now, in the laboratory, we can actually observe the physical process of how a message from the brain influences the immune system.

NEW FINDINGS, NEW CONCLUSIONS

From this overview, I think you can see that there is now much research to support the observations that state of mind influences the development and the course of cancer and other serious illnesses. In my opinion, the definitive research has been done to prove that the mind influences the body. Now I think the most important area to address is how the mind can be used to influence the body most effectively. During the past ten years, that subject has been the emphasis of my work.

I believe that the power of the mind goes far beyond what I first imagined. In addition, I believe that, beyond the body and mind, there is another aspect of healing that needs to be addressed: the spiritual aspect.

The dictionary defines *spirit* as the life principle, especially in humans, and the feeling and motivating part of our lives. Working with spirit means enhancing our connection with this life principle. It means asking questions about why we're here on this planet, and about our own unique purpose in life.

Our work with patients has demonstrated that health involves body, mind, *and* spirit. And while the mind alone can be used to influence the physical state, it is used most effectively when it is aware of spirit.

Spirit gives us resources that can't be reached through

traditional psychological approaches. It opens us to healing forces that go far beyond our current understanding of our own limits. And we can learn to bring that power into our own lives.

This conclusion is probably going to be just as difficult to prove in the laboratory as my first findings were. However, through our day-to-day experience, we have developed new methods of communicating and working with spirit, and I'm confident that what I have learned from my patients is valid. If it takes ten or twenty or one hundred years to prove it, that's okay with me. While the research continues, I'm going to pass along what I know to you.

Let me summarize what I have learned:

• Emotions significantly influence health and recovery from disease (which certainly includes cancer). Emotions are a strong driving force in the immune system and other healing systems.

• Beliefs influence emotions and, in so doing, influence health.

• You can significantly influence your beliefs, attitudes, and emotions, thus significantly influencing your health.

• Ways of influencing beliefs, attitudes, and emotions can be taught and learned by using a variety of accessible and existing methods.

• All of us function as physical, mental, and spiritual beings. All aspects need to be addressed in the broad context of healing, with a focus on the particular needs and predispositions of a person who is ill, and that person's family, community, and culture.

• Harmony—balance among the physical, mental, and spiritual aspects of being—is central to health. This applies not only to the health of the individual's mind and body, but also to his or her relationships: with self, family, friends, community, planet, and universe.

• We have inherent (genetic, instinctual) tendencies and abilities that aid us in moving in the direction of health and harmony.

• These inherent abilities can be developed and implemented in meaningful ways through existing techniques and methods.

• As these inherent abilities are developed, proficiency develops, as when learning other skills. The result is greater harmony and a better quality of life, which significantly impacts one's state of health.

• This learning also changes our relationship with death, whenever it may come, lessening fear and pain and freeing more energy for getting well and living life more fully today.

Before you either embrace these observations or dismiss them, I ask that you use this book to explore whether or not what I have learned is true for you. Draw your own conclusions based on your own experience.

Do not decide in advance that your current beliefs about the "spiritual" exclude you from this work. We treat a significant number of people who are atheists, and they are always able to find terms for their experiences that are comfortable and meaningful for them.

Remember also that I am not asking that you exclude what your doctors can do for you. In fact, most of our work helps people cooperate more actively with their treatment and with their health care team. But, I am suggesting you can go even further to influence your own health.

Because some of the concepts regarding the body/mind/spirit relationship may seem difficult at first, we are going to show how they are reflected in the experience of one long-term cancer survivor, Reid Henson. This is a man who was given a terminal diagnosis in 1979 and was told that there was no effective treatment for his cancer, yet he is alive and well today.

Reid's experience can teach us much about the dynamics of cancer. We can look both at why he got sick—and why everyone is vulnerable to cancer—and why he got well, building on an ability also shared by everyone. This is the perfect opportunity to explore and learn whatever we can that will shed light on the whole process of developing cancer and getting well again. We will do this not to the exclusion of studying what has been learned from the whole body of medical and scientific work on cancer, but in addition to it.

Reid is a very interesting cancer patient in that he has spent more than ten years studying his illness in relation to his life and to Life itself. For the past several years, he has been sharing what he has learned through a series of letters to cancer patients. In this book, you will be reading those letters, which are filled with ideas, insights, and practical suggestions. Following each group of letters, I will give you additional insights into Reid's recovery process, as well as other ideas and practical suggestions for dealing with cancer and the challenges illness presents.

Unlike statistical research that is open to interpretation by various experts, we hope to give you the opportunity to study illness and healing in a way that can be meaningful and useful in your situation. I have found that patients often best understand what they discover for themselves.

If you are questioning whether or not doing the work in this book will work for you, you are already moving in the direction of health. I hope you will remain curious until you discover whatever it is you need to know to influence the course of the illness you are experiencing, as well as to improve the overall quality of your life.

2

One Patient's Testimony

The Miraculous Healing
of Reid Henson

I first met Reid Henson and his wife, Jana, in 1979, in a
new patient session. Reid continued to correspond with me
after he completed the session, communicating his progress
and his problems, as well as his interest in what eventually
became his letter series to cancer patients. Having now
worked with him and observed his healing process for more
than ten years, I know his story well. Although I will tell
you about Reid from my perspective as a physician specializing in the treatment of cancer, I thought Reid should tell
you himself about his experiences with cancer.

REID'S STORY

In 1979 I was diagnosed with a rare form of cancer,
hairy cell leukemia, and I was told that I had, at most,
about two years to live. The medical community had no
effective treatment to offer me at that time. But before I tell

you about my cancer-related experiences, I'd like to say a little about my life before the diagnosis.

I was born in Gainesville, Florida in 1939, my parents' third son. Our family was of very modest means, and I lived in the same house until I was married. I went through school in Gainesville, and I graduated from the University of Florida in 1962, receiving a Master's degree in business. I had participated in the R.O.T.C. program and went into the U.S. Air Force shortly after graduation. Upon completion of my military obligation, I joined the finance staff of a major auto company in Detroit, where I gained extensive training and experience in applying computer technology to business challenges. Later I became a business consultant, specializing in the application of computers to marketing, sales, and distribution problems.

In 1975 I moved to Chattanooga, Tennessee, to work with a very large soft drink bottler. Basically, my job was to establish a management company to oversee bottling operations in several states. In the first year, I spent only thirteen nights at my condominium on Lookout Mountain (near Chattanooga). I had been divorced for several years, and at that point in my life, my work was a great escape for me. When I wasn't working, I spent my time exercising and participating in sports. I was in top physical condition for a man of forty. I was also dating actively.

As you might imagine, focusing on work, exercise, and romance absorbed most of my time and energy, so that I didn't have to think too much about my life, which had become complicated and stressful in the years preceding my move to Chattanooga. I had failed to recognize that I was still having emotional difficulties stemming from the death of my infant son more than ten years earlier, as well as from my failed marriage. I hadn't even begun to deal with these issues. Also, my first son from that marriage had become quite a problem for my ex-wife and eventually for me, too.

Before I moved to Chattanooga, when Rob was fourteen, he had spent a summer with me in Denver, Colorado.
His mother had found him very difficult to deal with, but
around me he seemed almost angelic—until near the time
for him to go back to his mom that fall. He asked if he could
stay with me in Denver. In fact, he pleaded with me, but I
insisted that he go back, thinking it impossible to have him
live with me, as I moved around and traveled so much of
the time. A few days before he was supposed to leave, I was
at work when I received a call from the police department.
They had my son in custody for beating up another teen-
ager. I was absolutely shocked by his behavior. I promised
to take care of the medical bills for the youth he beat up,
bailed my son out of jail, and put him on a plane back to
Atlanta, agreeing to bring him back to Colorado for a
hearing.

After returning to his mother in Atlanta, Rob's behavior went from bad to worse. Finally, after I moved to
Chattanooga, my ex-wife insisted that I take him again. I
was still traveling a great deal, so I knew I had to find some
way of giving him constant supervision. I enrolled him in a
private Chattanooga boys school with dormitories. After a
few months, he got kicked out. He was suspected of being
involved with drugs, but I just couldn't believe that was
true. He assured me of his innocence.

I enrolled him in another school, and he got kicked out
of that one, too. I couldn't figure out what was wrong with
him, and he couldn't seem to either. He'd say, "Dad, I'm
really sorry that I keep doing things that hurt or embarrass
you. I don't mean to. I don't know why I do it."

I want to describe just one episode to give you a feel for
what he and I went through. I had been away on a difficult
business trip one week when I returned to find my new
condominium, which had cost me my lif's savings to buy,
totally wrecked. It was obvious my son had hosted a wild

party in my absence, but he had not had enough consideration for me to clean up the mess, nor had he even been
concerned about hiding it in order to avoid a confrontation. I was stunned. It looked as if someone had stolen a
dumpster from behind a bar and emptied it right into my
living room. In addition, someone had punched holes
through the wall in several places. It took me several days to
find my son to confront him. At this time, he would leave
for days at a time, saying that he was staying with one friend
or another.

He seemed totally baffled as to how things could have
gotten so out of control, and so was I. As he had previously
done over and over again, he apologized and appeared to be
sincerely sorry for what he had done. More than once he
said to me, "Dad, I don't know why I do these things." And
more than once I responded, "Don't give me that crap. I
never did anything like this when I was growing up."

On another occasion, he called and asked if I would
meet him for a pizza after work, and I said, "Sure, I'd love
to." He didn't show up. Similar incidents occurred periodically thereafter.

Then he disappeared for months. During that time, my
emotions ran the full spectrum. I'd go back and forth from
being so mad at him that I'd want to kill him to being
genuinely concerned that he might be lying somewhere
hurt and afraid to call, or even dead. But eventually he did
come back, only to disappear again and again for extended
periods of time.

After hearing about my problems with my son, one of
our company's consultants who dealt regularly with alcohol
and drug abuse told me that this was the classic story of a
kid who's deeply involved with drugs. I didn't believe
him—Rob's behavior was terrible, but I thought he was just
a wild seventeen-year-old. I couldn't believe he was a drug

addict. However, as this man talked to me more, I could see that indeed my son had all the symptoms, and I had been blind to the possibility that drugs were part of his problem. I was clearly uninformed about such things at the time. Having already had him in counseling and having already tried to discipline him in every way I knew how, I called him in for a confrontation with our company's consultant. I offered my son several options—a one-way ticket to anywhere, enrollment in the military, a hearing before a judge for internment in a home or facility for incorrigible children, or participation in a drug treatment center. After he had considered the options for a few minutes and come up with numerous excuses as to why he couldn't take any of them, I insisted that he choose. He chose the drug treatment program.

I had a terrible, terrible time dealing with the fact that my son had become involved with drugs. I felt I had ruined his life, and I felt very guilty about it. I finally realized he had been crying out for help that summer in Denver and I had rejected him. I thought it was all my fault. I remember sitting in my condo on Lookout Mountain reading a magazine and seeing an article on leukemia. I thought to myself, "I deserve something like this for ruining the life of my son." But, as was my way at the time, I soon got busy with work and other activities, and tried to put such thoughts out of my mind.

During this period, I paid a lot of attention to my physical health, but I paid little attention to what was going on with myself mentally, and I gave no credence to spiritual matters whatsoever. This pretty well summarizes my condition as I entered into the cancer experience. Now there is no doubt in my mind that my inability to deal effectively with the stress in my life dampened my will to live and affected my health. The next few years were as difficult as any I have ever spent. On the other hand, they were also vitally interesting, exciting, and life-altering.

In October 1978 I entered a well-known clinic in Texas for my annual physical. I went there for an extensive checkup, and I passed the physicals with flying colors year after year. This time, I performed quite well in the various strength and endurance tests, but there were a couple of questionable items in my blood tests. I felt great, so I was not concerned, and neither were the doctors. However, a few weeks later, I noticed a dramatic drop in my physical endurance.

I kept records of how much exercise I did, so I knew, on a continuing basis, what sort of performance I had from day to day. I attributed the changes to just being tired or having a cold. Of course, I really didn't know what had made the difference, but I knew my endurance had fallen dramatically. This may have been the first tangible evidence of the cancer in my body.

In retrospect, it is interesting to me to note that the dramatic change in endurance occurred a few days after a very upsetting business experience. Basically, I felt totally mistreated after doing an excellent job with the best of intentions. I struggled greatly with issues of unfair treatment I perceived both toward myself and others. I remember thinking that life was getting more and more difficult for me.

Throughout the spring of 1979, I experienced one cold after another, and then the flu, and I felt run down and unable to shake whatever was plaguing me. I finally went to our company doctor, a local physician who came highly recommended. I thought he could help me get "back on track."

After numerous tests, this doctor presented me with some serious news. He wasn't sure exactly what the diagnosis was, but he told me that it could be cancer, and he wanted me to be evaluated by specialists.

Characteristically, I didn't plan to tell anyone else that my health might be in serious trouble. But there was one person I couldn't keep it secret from. For some time I had been steadily dating Jana, who later became my wife. It didn't seem that I could be around her so much without letting her know what was going on. She insisted on going with me when I went to the hospital for tests.

My doctor had referred me to a big teaching hospital, and there I encountered the most gruesome collection of people I had ever seen. The administrative personnel were disorganized, harried and unfriendly. In each of the waiting rooms, groups of sick people sat around in various stages of illness, along with their exhausted-looking relatives. Having rarely been sick before, I found this new environment most uncomfortable. I also had difficulty finding my way around—I'd go down one hall for one test, and then way down another hall for another unpleasant test. It was very confusing, very imposing, and very disagreeable.

One particular morning, Jana and I were summoned into a very small cubicle where a doctor was waiting. This was the specialist my local physician had first contacted, but I had never met him. He had a little table and a big file of test results. He was shuffling through the papers, looking very businesslike and preoccupied. All of a sudden, he jumped out of his seat, ran out into the hallway, and shouted to another doctor, "Hey, Rick, we've got another hairy cell leukemia here, and I diagnosed it over the phone—what do you think about that?"

That's how I found out I had cancer. It was an absolute shock to both Jana and me that any human being could be so insensitive that his primary concern was to brag to his fellow doctor about having diagnosed this on the phone. And there I sat—between a rock and a hard place. This was supposed to be one of the most skilled physicians in the field, and I needed his help with my health; but I just hated him for the way he treated me.

When he came back in, he sat down and proceeded to tell me that I had cancer, and unfortunately it was hairy cell leukemia, a terminal disease. He said he was surprised that someone my age (forty) had it, and remarked that since very few people had this form of cancer, no money was being applied to research it. He told me there was no reason to get my hopes up, that at best I had a couple of years or so. He also said that it probably wouldn't be the leukemia that killed me, but complications of pneumonia or some other infection. Then he summed up: "You know, I'd like to die playing tennis at ninety-five, chasing girls and having a great time, but this just isn't the way it always works. Sometimes problems arise, and unfortunately, you are the one who has this problem and the outlook is grim at best. Take your folder, go out to the desk. . . ."

And that was pretty much it.

My initial reaction was one of shock and burning anger, but not long after I heard the news, my mind went to something I had thought about the year before.

I remembered sitting in my condominium on Lookout Mountain, contemplating all my problems and thinking that I deserved to have leukemia for ruining my son's life. Was it just a horrible coincidence, or was there a real connection between that deep feeling of self-blame and my current diagnosis? Even though I had always strongly believed in the power of the mind, it was awesome and chilling to realize what it seemed I had unwittingly done. (Much later a psychologist agreed that my process had been dangerous indeed.)

This may seem a rather cold, analytical response to the news I'd received, but that was the way I dealt with problems in my life at that time. Not that I wasn't terrified at the thought of dying—I certainly was—but my natural tendency was to be very analytical.

By now it was the summer of 1979, and Rob was living with me again, after having gone through the drug treatment program and lived in a halfway house in Houston for a while. Unfortunately, his behavior was becoming more intolerable as the days passed. Once the diagnosis was confirmed, I let him know about it, hoping this would inspire him to be more considerate as well as more responsible for taking care of himself, as I had my hands full.

The people who ran the halfway house in Houston where he had stayed wanted to open a new halfway house in Chattanooga, so I helped them do that. At this point, I was still focusing my efforts on things outside of myself. I didn't know what to do for me, so I thought God might see that I was helping other people with this worthwhile project and give me some extra consideration.

I also continued working, thinking it best to stay involved with my job as much as possible. I did tell my employer about the cancer, as well as a few people who worked for me. I had some crazy thought going through my mind that if people saw me working even though I was dying of cancer, I would at least serve as a good example. It didn't take long, however, to see that I was killing myself by working full speed and not taking some action toward solving the problems in my life. I was very fortunate in these first couple of years that my boss and my staff were so thoughtful and considerate.

A month after the diagnosis, Jana told me she wanted us to get married. She said she wanted to be with me, to share with me any and all of the time I had left in my life. She said she was in love with me and willing to take on the challenge of helping me through this illness. She did not want to be with me as my girlfriend, however; she wanted to be my wife. She thought her life would be richer for being a part of this experience, no matter what happened.

I thought nothing could be crazier than getting married when I was supposed to be dying. Despite the fact that I had fallen in love with Jana, or even because I had fallen in love with her, I didn't think it was fair to bring her into this mess I felt I had created. On the other hand, I knew I needed help, and I did not want to tell my parents about my condition. Both were elderly, and I didn't see how telling them would be of any value. I was afraid that I might not be able to go through this alone, and Jana seemed genuinely interested in taking on the challenge. I entered into the marriage, as I think we both did, naïve about how big the challenge would be. We got married on September 1, 1979. Over the years, I have come to love and respect my wife from the very deepest levels of my being.

I invited Rob to take part in our wedding, and he continued to live with Jana and me after we were married. It wasn't too long, however, before I found drugs in his room, and the counselors at the halfway house strongly suggested that I ask him to leave. He left, but not without much anger on both parts.

I decided early on that I wanted to live, which in retrospect has proven to be one of the most vital decisions I made in my cancer experience, and one that I definitely consider a major turning point. I felt that since I had gotten myself into this situation, there was some way I could get myself out. I don't see it exactly that way today, but that's how I saw the situation then.

Although I had a tremendous fear of dying, the fear was not immobilizing, but stimulating—I saw myself moving quickly toward death unless I responded forcefully to move in the other direction. I had been in the consulting business for years. I was used to going into problem situations, gathering a lot of information, sifting through it, finding a solution, and then implementing the necessary steps to make it work. Since my methods had served me well in business, I was determined to use the same approach with cancer. I wasted very little time in gathering information and identifying some alternatives to just sitting around waiting to die.

Although I can't recall all the things I did, at least not in the exact order in which I did them, I can tell you about some of the areas I looked into and my thoughts about them now.

It was late in the fall of 1979 when someone gave me Dr. Simonton's book *Getting Well Again*. I read it with great excitement because it espoused beliefs very similar to my own. I called the Simonton Cancer Center, and Jana and I got into the next patient session that we could enroll in. The work we did there was the beginning of an intense effort to find a response to cancer that would work for me.

One of the best things about Dr. Simonton's program was that it gave me hope. Here was a doctor who knew at least as much as the specialists I had been to, and probably more. He had treated many cancer patients who had "terminal" diagnoses, and he thought I could live. Who was to say that he couldn't be right and my doctors wrong? He was saying what I wanted to hear, he was saying that there was a chance. In addition, he gave me some concrete tools for dealing with cancer. Some of the important things I took home with me were a two-year plan for regaining my health and the courage to ask for help from sources that I would not have considered before. And, most important, I took home an increased will to live.

I came back to Chattanooga and began to work regularly with a psychologist to deal both with the issues that had begun to surface as a result of my illness and with other personal problems that I had long ignored. I had never been to a psychologist or psychiatrist before, and I hadn't really understood the nature of their work. In fact, my initial reaction was, "I'm not crazy, I'm sick. I don't need a psychologist." Nevertheless, I found several local psychologists to be of great help to me, and I found that my new wife was quite willing to go along, as needed, and to work with me.

In addition to the psychologists, one of the first of many helpful people that I came across during my illness was a man who had once been a physician but was now what I guess most people would call a spiritual healer. I was introduced to him by the people who ran the halfway house I helped form in Chattanooga. They suggested that I call this man, but they were very vague about what he did. I took my time in contacting him, but finally, because my friends persisted, I agreed to call him.

When I called and told him who I was, he said, "Oh yes, I know about you," and then I told him a little about my illness. I was shocked when he asked me straight out, "Well do you want to live?" I said, "Yes, very much so." So he said, that being the case, he would work on it. He asked me just to try to be peaceful and not be worried or concerned. I thought the guy was nuts.

It was soon time for me to go back to the hospital for a checkup and more tests to see how the illness was progressing. I knew my doctors were very worried about my blood counts. I thought since the date for the checkup was approaching, I would call the healer back and see if he needed some more information or my medical records or something. I couldn't even begin to comprehend his being able to help me without seeing me, and my friends from the halfway house wouldn't even attempt to explain. So I called him again and told him about my concerns. He said he had been working on my behalf, and that when I went back to the hospital, there would be a tremendous change, a tremendous improvement. I didn't really believe it, but I told Jana what he had said.

We went back to the hospital, where I went through the appropriate battery of tests, and again the doctor called us to his office. He said, "Mr. Henson, are you taking any medicines or vitamins that I don't know about?" I said, "No." He said, "Are you doing some special exercises?" I said, "No." He said, "Are you doing anything out of the ordinary that you haven't told me about?" I said, "No." He said, "Well, there has been a miraculous change in your blood that I just don't understand. If this keeps up, you won't need us."

Jana and I looked at one another; then we left the office and went out and sat in our car in front of the hospital and cried for a long time. We cried tears of joy. We had an overwhelming feeling that this healer was a special person. It didn't make any sense to me. I didn't know what he did. But I knew that on my previous visit the doctors had told me very little if anything could be done for me, and then I had talked to some guy I didn't even know on the phone, across the country, and he told me that I was going to be better *and I was.*

The healer later sent me a series of lessons that inspired me to study my own mental processes. This personal exploration was tied in with Bible study and prayer work. For most of my life, I had wanted nothing to do with religion, but these things became increasingly important to me as time passed.

After this experience, I began to explore the work of many other types of healers. One of the local psychologists in Chattanooga occasionally sponsored a woman who came up from Atlanta to do psychic readings. I went to such a session and was amazed at her insights.

Not long afterward, I met another woman who was speaking in Atlanta about psychic healing. I was surprised to learn that she had taught alternative healing methods at a famous medical school. I couldn't verify that she had actually healed people, but she had been given credit for healing many cancers. Because of her experiences and insights, I asked her to work on me. We met about once a week for six months. The sessions often involved her simply placing her hands over me, or she might suggest something that I needed in my diet or some special exercise to do.

She once mentioned that her healing powers were greatly heightened around the pyramids in Egypt. When I found out that she was going to be in Egypt at the same time Jana and I would be traveling in Italy, I arranged to fly to Egypt for a healing session inside one of the pyramids. By this point, the summer of 1984, Jana and I had become friends with my local doctor and his wife, and we were traveling with them. I invited my doctor along to witness this healing session.

The healer never touched me physically, although throughout the healing session it felt as if she were touching me in a rather forceful way. In those spots where I thought I had felt her hands, there were red spots about the size of a pencil eraser. My doctor watched her every move and said that she had not put her hands on me. She explained that she worked through what is called the human aura or the human energy field. In any case, she said the process would revitalize my natural healing processes, which would then expel the toxins that had accumulated in my body. I don't know if it was a matter of purification, but afterward I was about as sick as I have ever been. I threw up from one end of Italy to the other. So I don't know if the healer helped me or hindered me, but as had happened when she had worked on me in the past, I had a rather dramatic physical reaction seemingly as a result of her work.

In addition to consulting healers, I also spent a lot of time reading about Edgar Cayce, one of the best documented psychics in American history. His files and studies are contained in a library in Virginia Beach, where there is an organization based on his work, the Association for Research and Enlightenment (A.R.E.). In essence, Cayce's wife would put him into a trance and he would diagnose the ailments of people who had contacted him. (Most of them he never met personally.) Then he would recommend some sort of therapy, which usually involved a natural process like a change in diet or exercise. When people implemented his suggestions, a large number of them got well. Thousands of such cases were documented.

Jana and I decided to participate in one of the week-long sessions at A.R.E. Afterward, we were even more impressed with the reality of spiritual healing. I didn't understand it, but I certainly came to realize that there were many aspects of healing that went far beyond today's traditional medical viewpoint.

For the next three or four years, I spent many hours studying the mind's effect on the body. I even enrolled in a local college and pursued a master's degree in psychology.

I read about people doing extraordinary things under hypnosis, yet I didn't have any confidence in the typical hypnotist. The ones I knew about were basically concerned with helping people change habitual patterns such as smoking or overeating. I felt my problems were profoundly different, and I decided that the local hypnotists probably didn't know any more than I did about using hypnosis to treat cancer. So I undertook my own program. I read several general books on hypnosis and self-hypnosis, and a psychologist gave me some ideas on adapting the information for my own use.

I then created some audio cassette tapes for myself. At the beginning of each tape, I read the steps for progressive relaxation from a book on hypnosis. At the end, I read the steps for bringing myself out of deep relaxation. In the middle I would give myself information that I needed in order to deal with a particular problem. For example, I might be feeling guilty about my son's drug addiction. I would write down all my feelings about the guilt and read this onto the tape. I then thanked my mind for having done the wonderful things it had done for me all my life. Then I said something like this: "I know that this is a difficult problem that I am faced with. Since you [my mind] have been an ally to me all my life, helping me with all my problems, I am now going to be silent and listen to whatever you have to give me in the way of guidance." I would then leave a period of silence, about five minutes or so, and listen for a response from my inner wisdom.

I found this a tremendously powerful method for probing into my subconscious. I learned a lot about my mental processes from doing this over an extended period of time.

In addition to hypnosis and progressive relaxation, I studied a number of related topics. For example, I became curious about voodoo. From my reading, I discovered that in certain parts of the world, voodoo appeared to have real life and death power over the people who believed in it.

I also read about the fire-walkers in Ceylon, who are able to walk barefoot across hot coals without injury. I thought about the fact that people in Chattanooga, where I live, are not able to do this. It seemed likely to me that the real differences were in our belief systems, which, in turn, were largely the product of our culture. Later, in talking with Dr. Simonton, I found out that, in less than one hour, he himself had learned to walk on red hot coals.

I read about Australian aborigines and their incredible tracking abilities. Through a process involving spiritual contact, they can follow someone's footsteps years after the steps have been obliterated by rain and sand.

I read books about various Eastern masters and studied, rather superficially, some of the Eastern religions. I invested in a mail order course in a type of yoga, and at one point was very interested in this discipline.

If nothing else, my readings proved to me that if I could find a book that claimed to be the truth about something, then I could almost always find another one that sought to prove the opposite. I became convinced that human beings could believe almost anything, and that what they believed had a lot to do with the course of their lives and health. And I observed that there were many things about mind and spirit that we had not yet come to understand.

In addition to alternative healing methods, I was also experimenting with more traditional therapies.

In 1980 my doctors advised me to have my spleen taken out to prevent it from rupturing, a dangerous possibility for someone with hairy cell leukemia. They assured me that it was a simple operation, and they recommended that I do it at a time when my blood counts were good, rather than waiting until they were low, when the operation could become necessary and risky. I decided that it was in my best interests to cooperate. The operation turned out to be quite an ordeal, but in any case, it prevented my ever having a ruptured spleen.

Early in my illness I also began taking vitamins. One relative, a former surgeon who had become unable to practice due to a leg injury, had become active in working with vitamins and nutrition. I had always been a big believer in vitamins, so I asked him to come up with a program for me. It seemed to me that in the natural process of fighting the cancer, my body might be using excessive amounts of one ingredient or another, which could create a chemical imbalance. If my body needed an extra supply of certain nutrients or vitamins, I could help myself recover by supplementing my diet. This is not a medical explanation, it is simply what I came to believe. In my opinion, vitamins were a great help to me.

Of course, the doctors at the hospital dismissed any possible effects of the vitamins, saying that all they did was make my urine more expensive. All I know is, I was expected to have a lot of colds and infections because of my low immunity, but I didn't. In fact, Jana mentioned several times in amazement that she had more colds than I did. Just as I did with other treatments, I later learned to ask my inner wisdom what I needed and took the vitamins I was guided to take.

Despite all this hard work and study, by the summer of 1981, two years after the diagnosis, I was not doing so well. Tests showed that the cancer was winning and I was losing. It appeared that the doctors were right when they forecast I would have only a couple of years to live. I began to work harder and harder, until I was spending literally all my waking hours fighting the disease and trying to figure out what to do.

My wife stood by me, supporting most of my efforts with understanding and enthusiasm. Occasionally she would try to steer me away from something that she thought was not worthwhile. At one point, she came to me and told me that I was spending so much time meditating that she was afraid she'd come home some day and find me wearing nothing but a diaper, with a turban on my head. After we talked about it, she agreed that I had to continue to do whatever I thought would be best for me, no matter how ridiculous it might seem to her or anyone else. I just can't communicate how much it meant to me to have Jana as my ally in the struggle to win the fight against cancer.

By August, I was very ill, and my son got into some very serious trouble. One day my ex-wife called to say that he had been locked up, this time by Federal authorities. She wanted me to come down to Atlanta and bail him out and get him an attorney. I was furious, and I was really fed up with Rob and all his problems. I felt it was time for him to pay for violating the law, just as I would have to if I were in his shoes. I didn't see how he could learn the lessons he needed any other way.

Through the work with my first healer, I had started a practice of praying about my problems. Now it was in praying about my son that I experienced an urge to write something down. I got out a pencil and piece of paper and wrote for some time. I felt I was in a different state of awareness than my normal, waking consciousness, and when I looked back at my writing later, I was unfamiliar with the message. This is part of what I had written:

I am the Creator of the heavens and the earth and all of the creatures living thereon. Yes, it is I who designed the reproductive processes in all living things. Know that I have preordained that your role would be exactly as it is.

Understand that you are an integral cog in the continuation of mankind in the earthly environment. You will do well to note, however, that you are but a part of my grand design. Does it follow, therefore, that you will claim ownership of the fruits of my labor? No, the children of the world belong to me.

Yes, I have called on you to play a special role in the lives of a few. But, I repeat, all the children belong to me. I have given each one a life and the freedom to do as he chooses with it. . . . Yes, you are free to offer your best guidance and direction to my children, but only with the clear understanding that each is free to pick his own path. . . . Soon they will assume command of their own lives, just as those who have gone before them.

The urge for freedom will soon come to pass in every life I give. Know this in advance and you will not be surprised. . . . None of you will have enough resistance to overcome the tremendous urge for freedom that will soon swell in each youngster's breast. *Do not try.* For I myself watch over my ever-developing children. At this point, your role is complete and I am pleased. . . . You will do well to not let your own vanity interfere. It will be at this point that it will be time for you to let go . . . and let me. For I am adept in this chosen role. You, on the other hand, have many other challenges to deal with and you must face them yourself. The same is true for your children. They must do it themselves.

I didn't know exactly what had occurred when I received this message. I had heard of "channeling" and "automatic writing," but I didn't know if this was either. What I did know was that I now somehow had the approval I needed to cut my son loose. I no longer felt guilty about his problems. I told my ex-wife that I would not bail him out, I would not send lawyers. I had cleaned up his messes for quite some time, and I was done. He could stay in jail. I also told her that I didn't want to hear from him if he did get out—no cards, no letters, no calls. He would just have to start taking responsibility for himself. I believe this is the most important thing I have ever done for Rob. I believe he grew up more in the few months following that incident than he had in the previous decade.

But my health continued to decline. I started focusing more on prayer and studying the Bible. Then on September

23, 1981, a remarkable thing happened that changed my life forever. In essence, I had a miraculous experience in which I was told by God that I would be well again. I will tell you about that experience in detail in the letter series, but for right now, all I want to say is that by January 1982, I was a healthy man. In fact, for the next two years, I was as well as I've ever been. My endurance was beyond my belief. I could run for so long, it became boring. People couldn't believe how much energy I had. It was hard for most of them to believe I was alive.

Nineteen eighty-two and 1983 were good years. I was in remission. I was back at work full-time. I felt like a new man. Much as I had been inspired to write the message about my son, I was inspired to start a series of letters to cancer patients in which I could relate all the things I had learned.

However, that miraculous healing was only the beginning of my understanding about God and life. I had much more to learn, and in 1984 I began to realize that the lessons would be provided through another episode of illness. I knew I was going to have a recurrence and I knew why: I had misunderstood the miraculous experience. I thought I had figured out a way to cure cancer by contacting God. I did not realize that this miracle was a gift. I was giving myself more credit than I was giving God. Sure enough, during 1984 I began to observe symptoms of the illness, and my doctor confirmed that I again had hairy cell leukemia.

Just before Thanksgiving of 1984, I became so sick that I was rushed to the emergency room. My doctor told me that anyone else with such low blood counts would have died, but for some reason, my body had adapted to this condition. I was given a massive amount of blood to save my life, but, as a consequence of the transfusions, I became blind. I was told the blindness occurred because my blood counts had gotten so low that certain capillaries in my body had begun to close up; as blood rushed into the area behind my eyes, blood clots developed, and the blood clots caused the blindness.

Gradually, the vision in one of my eyes began to clear up a bit, but I couldn't see well enough to get around in my own house. Over the next six months, I slowly regained my sight, but I found out what it is like to be blind, and I have been awed by the skill and courage of blind people ever since. This experience further underscored my belief that our response to the problems encountered in life is much more important than the problem itself, whether the problem is cancer or something else.

During that same fall, my wife's mother, who is a nurse and lived in Dallas at the time, saw an article on a research hospital in Dallas that was experimenting with a drug called interferon. I showed the article to my local doctor, who looked into the program and encouraged me to sign up as an experimental patient. I was against it in the beginning, but eventually he convinced me that this drug might be helpful to me. I didn't know it then, but when I got on the plane with Jana to go to Dallas in December 1984, most of my friends in Chattanooga thought they were saying good-bye to me for the last time.

I was accepted into the interferon program, and I checked into the hospital. I would be in the hospital for weeks at a time, and then I would check out and be treated as an outpatient while Jana and I stayed with her parents. One weekend when we were at their house, I saw an advertisement on TV about a Bible study course designed to build faith. I decided that faith was exactly what I needed at this time, so I ordered the course. When I went back to the hospital, I spent a lot of my time reading the Bible and doing the exercises in the workbook.

Although I was being given interferon, I had developed a problem with infections. They would give me strong dosages of antibiotics intravenously, the infection would clear up, they would unhook the antibiotics, and the infection would crop up again in another area of my body. The doctors were concerned that all the drugs I was taking were beginning to take a toll on the functioning of various organs, and they were running out of ideas as to how to control these infections when I could no longer take the antiobiotics. I was in desperate condition.

Then one day early in November 1985, after having worked in my "faith workbook" for a while, I drifted off to sleep while Jana was watching TV in my room. Suddenly, I came wide awake. I had had another miraculous experience. I had again been told that I would be well, but this time I was told when. I was told that my body would resume making normal blood cells on December 1, 1985. Since blood cells live roughly 120 days, I knew I should be well by April 1. Of course, this was in November, so April seemed a long way off. Nevertheless, I absolutely knew that I would be well, as I had experienced quite a few spiritual messages of this type by this time. I was ready to check out of the hospital.

We asked Jana's brother if he would drive us back to Chattanooga, and he agreed. Unfortunately, although getting home seemed to be what I really wanted to do, the two-day ride in the van was not good for my back. I had been lying in bed for most of three months, and following that with a long car ride left me with back problems that proved to be very difficult.

By April 1986 my blood counts were indeed in the normal range. Now that it really seemed I would live, Jana had time for a wish of her own: She wanted us to have a baby. The doctors had told me I was sterile from the treatments, but we decided to try anyway. In 1987 Jana conceived; unfortunately, she suffered a miscarriage due to a physical problem that she was unaware of before the pregnancy. The next year, however, she became pregnant again. On January 28, 1988, our healthy son, Clayton, was born.

Today, comparing where I am physically, mentally, and spiritually to where I was back in 1979, the most significant thing to me is that I am more than a decade older than I was when I was told I had a terminal illness. Physically, I am in good health, although I still have trouble with my back. (I no longer take any medications for the cancer.) My blood counts are taken only occasionally. They are usually well within normal range, although one count or another is sometimes above or below generally accepted guidelines.

Although my job is somewhat different, I still work as an executive in the soft drink industry. However, I look at my work as far less important than I once did. It's honest work; it provides me and my family with all the worldly goods that we need. But it is no longer an escape from life for me.

Jana and I still live in Chattanooga. The biggest change in family life for us was the addition of our son, Clayton. Since Jana and I both had physical conditions that might have precluded having children, we both feel he is truly an answer to our prayers. He has added immeasurable goodness to our lives.

I am also glad to tell you that my older son, Rob, has weathered his drug problems and is pursuing a career in music. Our relationship has improved dramatically, and he seems happy with his progress in life.

I want to be sure that you understand that his problems with drugs did not cause my illness. Instead, I now see my *response* as the problem—and I believe that our difficulties were a powerful stimulus for change in both our lives. It was a long time before I was sufficiently prepared to cope with such matters, but I see this lack of preparedness as a reflection of my own shortcomings, not his. As I see it, both of us needed help in dealing with the circumstances of our lives. Although we weren't much help to each other at the time, hopefully each of us has grown in understanding and can now be of service to others going through similar challenges.

Different people have different opinions as to which of the healing methods I used worked and which didn't—which contributed to my return to health and which had nothing to do with it. Whatever they think, I am the one who lived through all of this, and I have very firm views as to the causes of my survival.

I believe that each one of my experiences with alternative healing methodologies, as well as some of the more traditional treatments, were of value to me. I don't know how to explain why, but since I was told that there was no solution for me in traditional medicine, I felt that I had to find my solution outside of that realm. I don't know if this sort of exploration is necessary or even valuable to others, but I needed to explore these things to satisfy my own curiosity. The methods I have mentioned here are actually only a few of many I explored.

The greatest value of my extensive study and experimentation was that I ultimately did find a spiritual approach to life as the answer to my problems. When that solution to my cancer finally emerged, I knew it was right for me. I had explored many, many avenues to healing and I had gotten something from each of them, but none of the others proved powerful enough to overcome the disease.

I feel certain that if health experts were asked which of the methodologies were responsible for the changes in my health, they would give many different answers. I think that the psychologists and psychiatrists would feel that therapy was central to my getting well. I'm sure the surgeon would feel the splenectomy had a lot to do with it. Other doctors may feel the drugs were responsible. I'm sure that there are some who would conclude that the psychic healing sessions were important. I feel the vitamins were a contributing factor. And although each of these may have contributed in some way, if I had only one thing from my past experiences that I could go back to today, if I could choose only one, there is no doubt in my mind that the miraculous spiritual experiences I will tell you about in the letters are far more important than all of the others.

In stating this belief, I do not mean to demean the contribution of other aspects of my healing experience. I feel that faith, hope, and the will to live were a crucial part of the process. I would also say that traditional medical procedures gave me the time I needed to make the inner changes that resulted in the miracles I experienced.

I also want to be absolutely clear that I don't know what you need to get well. You may already have seen similarities in my life and yours, and certainly you have seen differences. Since no two of us are alike, I'm sure that you will need to find your own path to health, just as I did. I only hope that by sharing what I learned from my experiences, both your health and your life will benefit.

DR. SIMONTON COMMENTS

From the beginning, Reid's enthusiasm, deep interest, and the intensity with which he approached his situation made me believe he had a good chance of beating the odds and getting well. As you have read, Reid went far beyond the Simonton Cancer Center's program in his efforts, using it as a launching pad to an adventure in discovering life.

Many patients that I see are in the midst of trying a number of alternative healing treatments. Over time, my philosophy has become that I don't know what someone needs in order to get well. I see a certain form of treatment working for one person, while the same treatment proves to be a waste of time and energy for someone else. I neither encourage nor discourage people from trying a particular treatment. What I am interested in is helping them to develop a way of listening to their own inner processes that tell them which treatment to pursue. This ability to connect with our own source of wisdom takes time and patience to develop, and for many, the effort can become frustrating. But it is well worth it.

Like Reid, many people see what they need to do in order to move toward health. But unlike Reid, as soon as they begin to run into problems in implementing such changes in their lives, they become discouraged and give up. They may not have the inner strength or the support from others necessary to continue the work that has to be done. Reid and I hope to be able to help you obtain whatever you might need in order to heal your life—physically, mentally, and spiritually.

3

Beginning Your Healing Work

A Week at the Simonton Center

There have been some significant changes in the Simonton Cancer Center's program since *Getting Well Again* was written and since Reid and Jana Henson attended the patient session in 1979. The underlying philosophy is still very much the same: *Health is a natural process.* The techniques we use to move toward health still include imagery, meditation, working with inner wisdom, and goal setting. However, I have received very valuable feedback since I began this work in 1971, and I have altered the program accordingly. In addition to focusing on spiritual as well as mental processes now, I have refined the techniques we use at the Center considerably.

Two of the most valuable things that a person experiencing cancer takes back from our five-and-a-half-day session are the skills that will help them deal with a life-threatening illness and the emotional support of other patients. By the time you have completed the work in this book, you will have had the opportunity to learn every skill that we teach at our patient sessions—and more. At the end of this chapter, you will find a copy of our schedule, which indicates where to find the information and exercises for each of the sessions held at the Simonton Center.

While you won't have the benefit of sharing and learning from other patients who are just beginning this journey, you will have the example and support of Reid Henson, a patient who has been where you are and who is now where you probably want to be—enjoying good health.

In this chapter, I am going to review some of the general concepts of our program, as well as give you some ideas on how to establish a strong foundation for your healing work. This information, as well as the exercises presented in the next two chapters, will be helpful to you in working with the letter series. Please take some time to read these two chapters carefully and to do the exercises. If the concepts are new to you, you may find them difficult to understand at first. Don't expect to absorb each idea immediately—you don't need to "get" everything on the first reading. Basic concepts are repeated throughout the book.

THE SIMONTON CANCER CENTER

The Simonton Cancer Center's new patient sessions are held at a conference center in Pacific Palisades, California, which is just outside Los Angeles, near Malibu. This is a very special place, once a part of Native American sacred healing grounds. The members of the tribes who used to meet here prided themselves on being fiercely independent, yet they cooperated with each other. That is the same spirit we try to instill in our program participants. We hope that each patient and each support person will maintain his or her own fierce independence, yet cooperate with one another, with the other patients, and with our staff.

Upon each patient's arrival, we try immediately to help him or her feel safe, comfortable, and protected. This is an important environment to create for yourself in doing your own healing work.

Choose a special place or part of a room and gather together your meditation tapes, journal, photos, or whatever else you need to create a peaceful space without distractions. Create a regular time within your daily routine to do your healing work, and make sure that other people respect it. (You may need to be quite assertive about this, especially if you have small children.) This is a way to tap the power of ritual for your own personal learning.

In our orientation meeting at the Simonton Cancer Center, we cover some very basic guidelines for the week ahead that also apply to you in working with this book.

Let your desires and interests guide you in your healing work, and pay attention to the feedback you get from your body, as well as to your inner feelings. Let joy be your compass heading. If you are tired or don't feel well, let that physical or emotional pain be a signal to stop. Honor your limitations.

People come into our program with varying physical abilities. Some show almost no evidence of illness; they may just have been diagnosed, or they may be in remission. Others have very advanced disease. Many are undergoing full programs of standard medical treatment, in addition to the work they are doing with us. We never offer our program as a substitute for appropriate medical therapies. It is intended to support and enhance treatment, and to help patients discover their own individual path to healing.

Sometimes patients will look at another patient who is doing well—who may be actively exercising, for example—

and think, "I need to be doing what that person is doing." This is not the best approach. They need to be doing whatever they need to be doing. Don't base your work on another patient's abilities. You will find your own way of doing whatever you need to do in a way that is healthy for your unique situation.

Right now, I'd like you to take a moment to appreciate how you have been feeling, and to appreciate that despite your difficulties, you are making an effort right now—by reading or listening to this book—to improve your health. Know that you've been dealing with your illness the best way you know how. I want you to imagine yourself getting insights from this chapter, as well as from the letter series that lies ahead. Imagine that a broader understanding of your health is unfolding, and that you are beginning to understand how your life and your health fit together.

THE ROLE OF THE PRIMARY SUPPORT PERSON

Each patient who participates in the Simonton Cancer Center Program is asked to bring a primary support person along for the full five-and-a-half days. If the patient is married, the support person should be the patient's spouse. We want our work to help the marriage grow stronger, rather than cause more distance in the relationship. If the patient is not married, he or she needs to bring another support person. The primary role of the support person is to help the patient take the concepts back home and to be supportive in integrating the work into their home environment.

I think Jana Henson is a wonderful example of the effectiveness of an interested and enthusiastic support person. She participated in the new patient session with Reid, and over the years she has attended numerous seminars and lectures with him, read many of the same books, worked with him and his psychotherapist, and taken part in Reid's other efforts to get well with great enthusiasm. Most importantly, she did not do this at the expense of her own health. She took the time to apply the work to her own life, taking care of herself so that she would remain healthy and could continue to provide strong support for her husband.

I urge you to do the work in this book with your spouse or your primary support person. At the very least, ask them to read it so that they will understand what you are doing and how they can best help you. My first message to any person who is taking on the role of primary supporter is this: Do not attempt to help the cancer patient apply the work to his or her situation unless you are specifically asked to do so. Keep asking what you can do to help, but don't give advice. You want to be encouraging and you want to understand what the patient is attempting to do so that you don't work against him or her, but your primary focus needs to be on your own life. Take care of yourself. You need love and attention at this time, too.

If you don't have a primary support person, if you are single and living alone and have no family member or friend with whom you feel you can share this book, you can still do the work. I once had a patient show up at a session alone and in desperate condition. He had recurrent lung cancer with brain metastases. Of course, we didn't want to send him away, but he had to do the work on his own. To complicate matters, he had no money and could not afford to pay for a therapist when he returned home, and he had no support group in his area. Nevertheless, he put what he learned into practice and now, more than twelve years later, he is alive and well.

COMMUNICATING WITH YOUR SUPPORT PERSON: RESPONSIBILITY AND BLAME, GUILT AND FORGIVENESS

Throughout the week at the Simonton Cancer Center, we work to open up and improve communication between the patient and the primary support person. We provide a safe environment in which a lot of unspoken thoughts and feelings are aired for the first time. Usually both patient and support person are using a lot of energy to hold back things they haven't dared to say. Once one person in a group begins to speak with deep honesty, relief floods the room. People see that everyone is dealing with similar issues. They also see that the basics of good communication are the same for everyone.

For one assignment, we ask support persons to list those things they see the patient doing that they consider detrimental to his or her health, and also the things that the patient is not doing that they believe he or she needs to do. We then put the support people in a circle in the center of the room, and they discuss their concerns with each other, while the people they came with listen. There is a lot of honesty and sharing in this session.

One of the common feelings expressed by support persons is frustration. They are afraid that the patient won't get well, or that they won't get well quickly enough if they do only what they've been doing. They often want the patient to do things their way. They can become obsessed about small health issues—nagging the patient to eat more broccoli, for example. And all their love and fear may be hidden within this bossiness and advice-giving. We help them to express these emotions more directly.

Support persons also express a lot of guilt. We hear things like, "I was so focused on my work that I didn't give him enough love, and now he has cancer." Or, "I have been spending so much time with the family that he had to get cancer to get my attention."

It is very important for both the patient and the support person to confront and express feelings of frustration and guilt. Most of the time, it is helpful to then acknowledge that each of us does the best we can with the information and capabilities we have at any particular time. No one consciously forces a loved one to become ill, and none of us can be all things to all people and meet every need that others have.

As in any significant and healthy relationship, both patient and support person need to become skilled at negotiating needs. It is important for each person to begin to ask for more of what he or she wants, both from him or herself and from the other person. Each person needs to become very clear about his or her needs, and also to communicate those needs clearly and appropriately—in a way that the other person can best understand and act on them. For example, patients might tell their support person how to communicate advice when it is asked for, so that it comes across as support, not as an attempt to control.

We also hear a lot of resentment on both sides during this session. Statements like, "You made me sick!" Or, "If you hadn't been doing that, you wouldn't have gotten sick and made my life miserable!" That level of anger and resentment is common under the stress of illness, but it needs to be resolved. It can damage both the quality of life and the course of the disease. Depending on the level to which resentment exists in your relationship, you may need help from a therapist or a clergy member in dealing with this very common, but difficult problem. We suggest that our patients continue to do work in this area after they return home.

One of the ways we help patients and support people to deal with resentment, not only toward their partner but toward anyone in their life, is to work on forgiveness. The exercise we do at the end of this session may be helpful to you.

A Forgiveness Exercise

Write down the name of anyone who seems to bring up any feelings of resentment in you. Next to that person's name, write why you resent him or her. Then, going down your list one name at a time, close your eyes and imagine something good happening to each person—something you know he or she would especially like. Do this as often as resentful feelings about each person come up. In some cases, it will take many repetitions before your feelings change. You may find this difficult, but you will probably find that it lifts a great burden from you. (Remember that you are doing this exercise primarily for your health, not for the person you resent!)

After you finish this exercise, I suggest that you take a long break, coming back to the next section tomorrow or whenever you feel rested.

MESSAGES AND BENEFITS OF ILLNESS

Early in each session, we help patients begin to identify their individual patterns of vulnerability, including the events leading up to their illness. If you know what makes you vulnerable, you are well on your way to knowing what would make you strong.

Three very important areas for exploration are stress prior to cancer, secondary gains of the illness, and the message of the illness. I want to give you some general in-formation to help you to approach these topics; however, we will go into these subjects in greater depth in the letter series.

Considerable research points to stress as an important influence on susceptibility and resistance to cancer, as well as on the course of the disease itself. In our program, we begin by identifying stresses six to eighteen months before the onset of cancer.

Sometimes people find it difficult to label stress, so I suggest you do this: Starting with eighteen months ago today, list any major changes that have taken place in your life. Has someone in your family been ill? Has there been a death in the family? Have any of your friends died? Have you changed jobs? Retired? Have you been laid off or fired? Has any other change taken place at work—even a major promotion? Have you moved? Have your children moved away from home? Have you divorced? Married? Any signifi-cant change—good or bad—during the past eighteen months should be on your list.

Whatever the change, the onset of illness may be an indication that you are not able to deal effectively with the stress of that change. Other people may be able to, but you are not "other people." At this time in your life, certain changes may also be more difficult to handle than they have been previously. Take a moment to recall Reid's story: In the few years before the diagnosis of cancer, he had changed jobs, moved, divorced, and his son had developed a prob-lem with drugs. The sum total of those events represented tremendous stress in Reid's life.

It may help you to go beyond the past eighteen months and take a look at other illnesses you've had. Try to re-member the stresses that preceded them. I'm very much aware of my own patterns. If I develop a cold, for example, I can be sure that I have overcommitted myself; I have too many things to do, I am not asking for help, and I am thinking that if anything is to get done, I have to do it. I am overburdened, overworked, and not playing enough. And so I am vulnerable to a cold virus that I might otherwise have shaken off easily.

Today we have identified many factors that contribute to cancer—inborn genetic tendencies, smoking, overexposure to the sun, certain lifestyle choices, environmental hazards, and so on. Stress is never the only factor in the development of cancer, and it varies in importance from one person to another. But once the cancer is diagnosed, it is the factor that we can do the most about.

One theory of cancer, called the "surveillance theory," says that we may in fact get and defeat cancer many times during our lives. The body develops abnormal cells, but the immune system destroys them before they multiply enough to be dangerous. But if our immune system is depleted by stress, our defenses fail and a cancer develops.

To go back to my cold—once I'm sick, I get rid of some of the burdens I'm carrying, get help with my work, and start playing more. I call these the "secondary gains" of having a cold. But once I've recognized the gains or benefits of having a cold, I can get those benefits for myself without having to get sick to get them.

Similarly, I ask patients to take a look at how cancer may be helping them deal with stress. What would you say are some of the secondary gains of your cancer? When I first raise this question, many people are shocked. What could be good about cancer? But then we take a deeper look together. Among other things, cancer can allow you to say no to yourself or to others in regard to things that you don't want to do. It can allow you to say yes to important parts of yourself that you have previously denied. Cancer can bring you love and attention from others. With cancer, limits and rules become suspended; all of a sudden there may be great freedom to refocus your life in many different ways.

I think of this need to refocus as the great message of cancer. Over and over again I have seen cancer as the body's way of shocking a person into making changes. I really stress that in our patient sessions. It is a hard concept to accept. Most people in our culture think that having cancer is terrible luck, a meaningless, random blow of fate. A few, like Reid at the beginning, feel they are being punished for some past mistake or transgression. But I believe that the message of cancer is always a message of love.

I believe that cancer is a message to stop doing the things that bring you pain, and start doing the things that bring you joy—things that are more in line with who you are and what you want your life to become.

Psychologist Lawrence LeShan writes about the deep hopelessness of trying to be who we are not. When we try to go against our nature, life doesn't work smoothly. Our response is often to try harder, but the harder we try, the farther we get from what we truly want and need. Our patients often experience a deep sense of relief in hearing this message. They need this permission to give up their rigid and inhuman expectations of themselves.

There are many different paths to experiencing the message of cancer, and we will explore them throughout this book. In the meantime, give some consideration to how you are handling the stresses in your life. Can you approach them in another way? Do you need some help you are not asking for? If you are having difficulty recognizing your stresses, look back at Reid's story. Can you see any similarities in his life and yours?

If you are beginning to recognize some of the secondary gains of your illness, don't apologize for them! Right now, go ahead and use your illness as an excuse to say no to things you don't want to do, and to try new things. Pay attention to what those things are. Take notes. This is a positive step towards honoring your real needs.

This would be a good time to take a break from reading and do some work on your stress list (page 52), if you haven't already. Afterward, do something pleasurable!

WORKING WITH A THERAPIST

I think it is a healthy decision for both the cancer patient and the primary support person to enlist the aid of a counselor, but this is especially important for the patient. During our patient sessions, we assign each couple a therapist. The therapist meets with the cancer patient and the support person, individually and together, at the beginning of the week, the middle of the week, and the end of the week. The therapist provides support during our intensive exploration of the psychological aspects of cancer.

If you are looking for a therapist to help you deal with your illness, find out if he or she has experience with mental/physical approaches, or with the spiritual/mental/physical approach we are using in this book. It doesn't matter if the therapist has not been trained at the Simonton Cancer Center. If the therapist is doing good therapy, he or she will have a good reputation in your community. If your doctor doesn't know of someone, you can go to your local hospital's oncology department and speak to an oncology nurse, social worker, or anyone who works closely with patients, and ask for recommendations. When you go to your first meeting with the therapist, take a copy of this book (or *Getting Well Again* or Bernie Siegel's *Love, Medicine and Miracles*) and say that you are interested in attempting to get well along these lines. Ask if he or she can help you do that.

Take care to evaluate your therapy. Is it helpful? Do you feel better after a session? Do you feel more confident about your ability to get well? You want to take all of these things into consideration. If you believe it isn't working for you, trust your judgment and find another therapist. This is not to say that some of the work in therapy is not going to be difficult; it probably is. But how do you feel after you've done that difficult work? Respect your feelings and maintain your personal integrity.

One of the things that Reid decided to do while attending our center was to seek the help of a local therapist when he returned home. You'll remember that at first he believed he didn't need a psychiatrist or psychologist, because he was sick, not crazy. Yet he found that his therapist played an important role in leading him to health.

SUPPORT GROUPS

Many patients also find comfort and help through a cancer support group. While such a support group was not available to Reid at the time he was in crisis, there are now numerous support groups around the country, with several to choose from in most urban areas.

You can evaluate the value of the support group for yourself much as you evaluate your therapy. Again, simply pay attention to your experience with the group. How do you feel before you go to the group session? How do you feel when you're there? How do you feel when you go home afterward? If you feel uplifted and motivated, wonderful! If, on the other hand, you leave home feeling okay and come back feeling lousy, then something unhealthy is going on, and you need to stop going until you can figure out what.

This doesn't mean that you shouldn't encounter any pain or grief, but if the leadership is good and the group is functioning well, your overall sense will be positive. If it is not, that doesn't mean that you can't use a support group; it just means that you need to spend a little time investigating the best one for your needs.

Enlisting the assistance and support you need may require particular attention if it goes against the grain of your personality—if you tend to be very independent or reserved and have always shied away from asking for support, as so many of our patients have. I urge you to lay this groundwork carefully, putting a support system in place as you begin this work, so that you are operating from as strong a foundation as you can reasonably create. We will come back to this several times in the book.

AN OVERVIEW OF THE WORK AHEAD

The work we do with patients at the Simonton Cancer Center revolves around the basic premise that cancer is a message of love. If a significant part of the cause of cancer is trying to be who we are not, then healing cancer involves opening to who we are. Our patients have told me that the work we do together gives them "a gentle mirror" to truly know themselves.

Here is an outline of the process:

1. Decide to get well. Make the decision to do whatever you need to do to get well, knowing that this will take you in the direction of joy and away from pain—both physical pain and mental pain.

2. Decide to open to who you are, and in doing so, allow yourself to be directed by desire and joy and guided by the wisdom that resides within and around you.

3. Develop trust in yourself, trust in others, trust in God, and in all there is. You can nurture your relationship with yourself by acting with integrity; this will also nurture your relationship with others and your relationship with all there is.

4. Ask for help. Open yourself to accepting help. In doing so, watch for preconceptions about where and from whom you can expect help. Don't limit yourself to the information you have right now. Stay open to new sources.

5. Become more aware of your thoughts and feelings of guilt, blame, and failure. Taking responsibility for your health does not mean you are to blame for getting ill. It does not mean you are a failure if you don't improve as much as you think you should. (Later, I will give you a specific process for dealing with such feelings.)

6. At the same time, move in the direction of accepting more responsibility for your life, your health, and your happiness. You are not the sole creator of your reality, but you are its co-creator. Experience how much you can affect your universe.

7. Feel and acknowledge your emotions, and learn to express them in ways that are appropriate for you and that maintain your personal integrity.

8. Actively participate in the healing process with aliveness, with positive expectancy, and with enthusiasm.

9. Develop the attitude of loving, alive curiosity.

10. Hold high thoughts. Think about things that are mentally, emotionally, and spiritually uplifting or comforting to you.

This is an overview of what we teach our patients, not a things-to-do list. These ten actions stimulate the healing process and bring a person closer to physical, mental, and spiritual balance. The work in this book will help you to take the steps suggested. The exercises in the next chapter will help you get started.

LISTENING TO FEEDBACK

If you haven't already done so, take a moment to appreciate the fact that in doing the work in this book, you're going to run into some difficulties with certain people in your life.

As you start to make changes and do things differently, you are bound to encounter resistance. Yes, some people are going to be excited and enthusiastic about your approach to your illness, but others are going to be anything from frightened to inconvenienced. Those people won't be much help to you; in fact, they may even try to stop your progress. This is often true in business relationships, especially if you have always been the good guy, the person people could overload with work, the person who could be counted on to stay late and come in early. When you start saying no because you have work to do around the cancer you are experiencing, you may find that people in your office get upset. Just be aware of that possibility, and stay focused on your priority— your health.

You will almost certainly encounter resistance from some family members. If you have been the mainstay, always willing to help, even "too good to be true," as so many of our patients have, people will be uncomfortable when you start to assert your own needs. Adolescents are often

the most threatened and resentful. They are already frightened of losing you, and they want you to stay just the same.
The husband of one of our patients expressed his discomfort
more subtly. "I just want my sweet wife back," he would say.
One day his wife looked him in the eye and replied, "If she
comes back to life, I die."

It is very difficult to explain the concepts of the work we
are doing together, especially to people who have no back-
ground or experience in this area. My suggestion is, don't
even try. Suggest that they read the book if they're really
interested. If you are unable to explain this work to someone else's satisfaction, the experience will tend to weaken
your confidence in your ability to get well. These situations
are best avoided by planning how to respond so that people
can find their own answers, while your learning and discovery process is adequately protected.

OTHER PRACTICAL GUIDELINES

Reid took some practical steps early in his cancer experience that helped him with his work and lowered his stress
level. As his illness became known, he wrote a letter to all
of his friends and colleagues, asking them not to inquire
about his condition every time they saw him. Reid found
that he could be having a perfectly nice day, not thinking at
all about leukemia, until some well-meaning person, seeing
him in the elevator at work, would say how sorry he was to
hear about Reid's illness, and ask how he was doing. This
forced Reid to repeat his health status over and over again,
and he found that discouraging. In his letter, he suggested
friends call his wife or his secretary to ask about his health,
and otherwise just wish him a nice day when they saw him.
This system worked well for Reid.

I know other patients have found telephone calls from well-wishers burdensome. It seems that many people have a frightening story about cancer to tell you, or they find your cancer terrifying and don't hide that very well. It's sometimes difficult to deal with these calls, especially when the callers are close friends or family members. Other than writing a letter, another response might be to buy a telephone answering machine and make good use of it. Record whatever message you want. You can tell them you're busy working on your health and when you take a break, you'll give them a call back, or say you are not taking calls today, or ask them to call someone else for information or to leave a message.

Here are several examples:

> Hi, this is Betty. If you are calling to find out how chemotherapy went today, it was fine, but I'm feeling a little tired so I'm staying away from the phone. Thanks for calling. Please leave a note of encouragement at the sound of the beep.

> Hi. You've reached Jack's telephone answering machine. Jack will be at St. Mary's Hospital for tests until Friday, and he'd love it if you'd call him there at 555-9989, room 123. Or, you can leave a message, since he'll be checking the machine for calls. Thank you. Please wait for the beep.

> This is Al speaking. I'm resting right now, but I'm doing just fine. You can call my friend Jane for the details. Her number is 555-2222. That's 555-2222. Please leave a message, and please be patient in waiting for me to return your call. Thanks for all your good thoughts.

If you don't want everyone from your office calling, ask one person at the office to keep everyone else posted on whatever you want coworkers to know.

On the other hand, you may be the type of person who wants phone calls. If so, ask people to call you. Otherwise, some of the people you most want to hear from may be hesitant to call. Ask your office to have one person call you each day. Ask your family to take turns calling you so that you're sure of a phone call every day.

On days when you are undergoing treatment, try to plan something nice to do for yourself afterward, so that your whole day isn't focused around what you may consider an unpleasant undertaking. Don't make one day chemotherapy day; make it the day you get chemotherapy then take the afternoon off to paint, read, or watch a movie. Don't make the day more difficult. Don't go to chemotherapy and then come home and pay bills. Don't go in for a checkup and then go by to see your CPA about your income tax because she's in the same neighborhood as your doctor. Plan something you like to do on days that you know may be tough.

As you begin to feel better, many people are going to come to you and ask you to counsel other cancer patients. They're going to ask you to drop by the hospital and talk to a friend who needs your help, or they're going to ask you to call someone and tell them how you got better.

Be careful about counseling other cancer patients. You need to continue to focus your energy on yourself. That doesn't mean that you can't help, but you may have to help in a different way. When someone asks you to talk to a friend with cancer, simply explain that wouldn't be the healthiest thing for you to do right now. Then give that person the name and phone number of a therapist you know who works in this field, or suggest the friend read this book or other books that you have found helpful. That's how you can help other cancer patients without harming yourself. Do this unless, after quiet contemplation, you feel led to talk to someone. Then the source that is leading you will be there to help you. But never offer help just because you think you "should."

In general, take a second look at your need to help anyone at this time. Remember that Reid involved himself with the halfway house right after his diagnosis. He later realized that he was mistakenly focusing his attention on external problems rather than putting his efforts into his own life and health. Stay focused on yourself right now.

SUMMARY

Although I have covered only general concepts and some simple practical suggestions in this chapter, the information you have been given is important in creating a solid base for doing the work ahead. Please ask yourself the following questions:

- Have you created a special time and place for doing your healing work each day?
- Have you involved your primary support person in your work?
- Who makes up your support team? What role would you like each person to play?
- Have you given some consideration to using a therapist to help you?
- If you are using a therapist, what do you think about the work you've done so far?
- If you have joined a support group, how do you feel before and after you attend the sessions?

- Have you identified the stresses/changes that have been a part of your life during the past eighteen months?
- How have you decided to handle questions from friends and family about your health?
- As you get better, how will you handle requests to visit other patients?
- What have you done to reward yourself for the hard work you've been doing to get well?

Your answers to these questions may be helpful in evaluating whether or not you are ready to proceed with the next chapter. You may believe you need to spend more time setting up your healing program, or you may believe you need to move ahead. Let your feelings and your energy level determine your schedule, and move ahead at your own pace, whenever you feel comfortable.

Simonton Cancer Center
Patient Session Schedule

DAY	SUBJECTS COVERED	WHERE TO FIND INFORMATION COVERED AT THE SESSION IN THIS BOOK*
Sunday	General information about the program	Chapters 1 and 3
Monday	Meditation and imagery The mind–body connection	Chapter 4
Tuesday	The two-year health plan (purpose in life, play, meditation, nutrition, support, exercise)	Chapter 5 Letter 9 and comments
	Meaning of illness	Chapters 3 and 4 Letters 1, 4, 5, 6 and comments
Wednesday	Support systems The primary supporter Family support systems	Chapter 3 Letter 15 and comments Letters 13, 14 and comments
	Medical support	Letters 16, 17, 18 and comments
	Therapy Support groups	Chapter 3 Chapter 3
	Inner wisdom, hope, and trust	Chapter 4 Letters 1, 4, 5, 6, 7 and comments
	Responsibility, guilt, and blame Support person	Chapter 3 Letters 2, 3, 18 and comments
Thursday	Death	Chapter 4
	Recurrence	Chapter 1 Letter 19 and comments
Friday	Staying well	Chapters 3 and 6

*Primary sources are listed; however, these topics are repeatedly discussed throughout the book in the context of related subjects.

4

Working with Imagery and Inner Wisdom

Power of Mind, Power of Spirit

Imagery is one of the oldest forms of healing existing on the planet. By "imagery," I mean the images produced by all the workings of the imagination, both conscious and unconscious. I have studied and researched using imagery for health for more than twenty years.

Your imagination has already played an important role in your illness. Reflect back upon your experience in receiving the diagnosis and the ensuing discussion regarding treatment and prognosis. What were your thoughts? What were your feelings? Were you primarily hopeful, imagining recovery? Or were you more fearful, dreading what was to come? The chances are that you experienced a combination of images, positive and negative, healthy and unhealthy. And all affect your body at the cellular level.

These images are related to your beliefs about the nature of your illness and treatment in general, as well as related to your beliefs about what your personal experience and treatment will be. Remember, the beliefs that trouble us the most are often based on our interpretation of facts, not on the facts themselves. You can learn to change your frightening or unhealthy beliefs and replace them with healthy beliefs. This will help you to get well.

How can you tell if what you believe is healthy? There are many ways, but the method we use with our patients was created by C. M. Maultsby of Howard University Medical School. He developed a simple, five-question test for evaluating the relative health value of any belief.

Ask yourself:

1. Does this belief help me protect my life and health?
2. Does it help me achieve my short- and long-term goals?
3. Does it help me resolve or avoid my most undesirable conflicts (whether these conflicts are within myself or with other people)?
4. Does it help me feel the way I want to feel?

And when appropriate, also ask:

5. Is the belief based on facts?

If you can answer yes to three or more of these questions, then the belief you hold is considered relatively healthy. If there are fewer or no yes answers, it is important you change your belief to a healthier one.

The reason we pay so much attention to beliefs in working with cancer patients is that beliefs create emotions and, as we have seen, emotions are an important driving force in the immune system and other healing systems. Healthy images increase your sense of power, well-being, and peace of mind. They strengthen your sense of connectedness with your inner wisdom, with others, with the world and the universe. And they help to keep your immune system in top working order.

Neutral emotions—feelings of calm, peace, and tranquility—also have a healthy effect on the body's healing systems.

Prolonged negative emotions, however, have an unhealthy effect.

A PLAN FOR CHANGING BELIEFS AND DEVELOPING GREATER EMOTIONAL MASTERY

The most effective time to work on your beliefs is when you are experiencing emotional pain, because then the unhealthy beliefs will be easier to identify. It will be clear that your undesirable emotions are interfering with your life—for example, if fear is interfering with your sleep. Here is a process for working on your beliefs.

Step #1   Identify the undesirable emotion you are feeling. (I will use fear in the example that follows.)

Step #2   Take a piece of paper and draw a line down the middle from top to bottom.

Step #3   In the left-hand column, list five or more beliefs producing the emotion.

Step #4   Evaluate each belief with Maultsby's questions.

Step #5   For the unhealthy beliefs, write out healthier incompatible beliefs in the right-hand column.

Step #6   Keep the paper with you, and when you feel the undesirable emotion, pull out your list and read it. (You may need to do this two to twenty times a day.)

Step #7   In addition, three times daily in a calm, relaxed state, using your breathing to help you relax, imagine the healthier beliefs. Do this for at least three weeks, or until the new beliefs become your new unconscious attitudes.

Here is the list written by a woman who arrived at the Center with far-advanced breast cancer. She was undergoing chemotherapy, but her health was deteriorating, and she was consumed with fear for herself and her only child, a six-year-old daughter.

FEAR

1. I'm going to die within two years and leave my daughter, regardless of what I or anyone else does.	1. I may or may not be alive in two years, and what I do makes a significant difference.
2. I'm going to be very sick and incapacitated, a burden to myself and others.	2. I may or may not be ill, and what I do makes a significant difference.
3. All of my unhealthy beliefs and feelings are making me worse, and I can't change this.	3. All of my unhealthy beliefs and feelings are making me worse, and I can change them.
4. I may be able to get well, but I would never be able to maintain my health and keep the cancer away.	4. I can get well and I can maintain my health and keep the cancer away.
5. I need to hurry up and make these changes, but I don't have enough time, especially since I don't know how to do it.	5. I have all the time I need to make the changes I need to make, and I know what to do *today!*

| 6. It's doable, but I can't do it. | 6. It's doable, and I can do it. |

Her list revealed not only her fears about the cancer, but also her fears about "failing" to improve her mental and emotional state in time. As she worked on her healthier beliefs with her husband (who was, in fact, devoted to her and her daughter), her hopelessness and agitation began to decline, she slept better, and she felt stronger than she had in a long time.

Notice that we do not use the term "positive thinking." Instead, we talk about "healthy thinking," or "healthy beliefs." This is an important distinction.

The biggest difference between "positive" thinking and "healthy" thinking has to do with the factual aspects of the belief. For example:

Unhealthy thinking   I will be dead within two years regardless of what I do.

Positive thinking   I will be alive and healthy two years from now.

Healthy thinking   I may or may not be alive two years from now, and what I do makes a significant difference.

As we can see in this example, positive thinking is healthier than negative thinking. The problem is that positive thinking doesn't necessarily align itself with the facts of nature or with real life. We are attempting to develop beliefs based on fact. Healthy thinking is aligned with reality.

Can you look back now at Reid's experience and see how his life and health changed over the years as his beliefs changed? His mind was deeply entrenched in some very unhealthy processes at first—for example, when he believed he deserved his leukemia for having ruined his son's life. However, by working with his beliefs and being open to change, he eventually came to believe that his son's experiences motivated him to move toward health. Note that Reid couldn't change what had happened to his son, but he did change his beliefs about what had happened. This change in Reid's thinking took place over a number of years, and it occurred after Reid had spent an enormous amount of time working on his beliefs on a very deep level.

Now I would like you to take a look at your own beliefs about your illness and your treatment. Take a few moments to write down what you believe to be true about cancer in general, and about your particular diagnosis and your chosen treatment. Then use the five questions to evaluate your beliefs.

You are not alone if your beliefs are unhealthy. Our general cultural beliefs about cancer are quite unhealthy, as well as our beliefs about treatment and the body's ability to heal itself. Culturally, we are taught that cancer is a strong disease that devours us from the inside out. Treatments are believed to be harsh and of questionable value. We have little confidence in our body's ability to heal itself. All of these beliefs are unhealthy and are not factual.

I am going to help you begin to change your beliefs about cancer by giving you three central beliefs about cancer that you can begin to work with:

1. The body has a natural ability to heal itself and overcome cancer. When cancer cells and normal cells are put together in the laboratory, cancer cells have never been demonstrated to attack or destroy normal cells. Never! However, under the same conditions, white blood cells routinely attack and de-

stroy cancer cells. Cancer itself is composed of weak, confused, deformed cells.

2. Medical treatment can help your body to heal itself, making it your ally in getting well.

3. Cancer is feedback that indicates a need for change—that you need to do more of the things that bring you joy and fulfillment, and fewer of the things that result in emotional pain; that you need to learn to respond to the stresses of life in healthy ways. This message is one of love. Acting on it can help you to align yourself with your true nature and significantly influence your body's ability to eliminate the cancer.

When you begin to learn a belief that conflicts with an old belief, the new belief often feels "wrong" at first. This experience is so common that psychologists have a formal term for it—"cognitive-emotive dissonance"—which simply means that your feelings have not yet caught up with your thoughts. This feeling of "wrongness" continues until the new belief becomes an unconscious attitude. It is important to realize that it is natural to experience these uncomfortable feelings. It's a little like going to England and driving on the left side of the road when you've only driven on the right side before. It feels "wrong" and very uncomfortable at first, but with practice, you gradually feel comfortable and can drive with little conscious effort.

The same thing will happen as you work to change your beliefs about cancer. At first you may feel that the work is very frustrating and artificial or, as our patients sometimes say, "phony." But gradually the new beliefs will become part of your unconscious attitude, and you will find that healthier images and thoughts emerge with little effort.

Meditation or the conscious use of imagery is essential in making these changes. It is the basic tool for intentionally creating new beliefs and developing them into unconscious attitudes. Although meditation or imagery is used for relaxation and pleasure, it can also be the process by which you make concrete changes in your health and your life. We'll begin by using your imagination to change your beliefs about your illness, treatment, and your body's ability to heal itself.

MEDITATION AND IMAGERY

I strongly suggest you approach the meditation exercises in this chapter in the following way: As you come to each meditation exercise, read it once straight through. Then do the meditation exercise once (I'll explain how later), write down anything you want to remember, and stop your work for the day. The fifth meditation exercise in this chapter is optional.

After you have worked through each meditation once, select the exercise that you believe best addresses your immediate needs and work with that exercise, and only that exercise, using it to meditate one to three times a day, for a period of ten to fifteen minutes, for as many days as it takes you to feel comfortable with it. Then you can start working with the other meditations, depending on your needs and desires. You will notice that each meditation has the same breathing exercise to help you get into a relaxed frame of mind. You can use this breathing exercise anywhere, at any time you feel a need to calm yourself.

Allow yourself six to eight weeks to develop the habit of meditating on a regular basis. Adjust the meditations you do to suit your needs, and continue to adjust the number of times per day you meditate and the length of your meditations until you develop a system that feels right for you.

If you've never meditated before, please don't worry

about how to meditate. It is a simple process that anyone can do. Remember, you have always used your imagination. You may want to have someone read or tape record each meditation for you, or you may want to do that yourself— many people find that the sound of their own voice on tape is very helpful. Reid spent a lot of time making his own recordings.

There are hundreds of books, as well as audio and video tapes, on meditation. If you are interested in this subject, you will have little trouble finding information, and I do think that it is healthy to explore various other methods after you've worked with these basic meditations for six to eight weeks. I suggest that you keep your primary form of meditation consistent and experiment with a new form no more often than every third meditation. In the meditation exercises in this book, we start the relaxation process by consciously breathing and relaxing the body, starting at the head and going down to the toes. If you'd rather start at the toes and move up toward the head, simply adjust the meditation as you record it.

I currently meditate one to three times a day, for about fifteen minutes each time. For me, meditation is a priority, so this is how I generally start each day. At one time, Reid spent many hours a day in meditation, and he still meditates for a short time each morning.

If you are highly motivated and practice any one of the meditations in this chapter three or four times a day for ten to fifteen minutes, you will very likely see progress in three to six weeks—you will begin to notice positive or neutral emotions emerging from your new and healthy beliefs.

The first meditation given here will help you begin your healing work by helping you to create images based on the three central healthy beliefs about cancer.

I suggest that you simply find a quiet place, letting those around you know that you need to be undisturbed for a period of time. It may be best to sit rather than lie down, so that you don't go to sleep. Sitting in a comfortable chair is fine—it is not necessary to sit on the floor with your legs crossed, or in any other special position. Adjust the temperature in the room to whatever makes you comfortable.

Whenever you meditate, keep the images simple. Simplicity will help you stay focused. The more complicated the images, the more scattered your focus, making the imagery less intense and less effective.

It is also important to be patient with yourself. If you've never meditated, you may find it difficult at first, so give yourself time to learn the process and to appreciate the value of it. Try to remain curious about what meditation can do for you, and try to be aware of any preconceptions that this just won't work. Experiment with it. See how it works for you. Basically, it is simply a tool for health, a way to change your beliefs and emotions so that they can help you get well.

Meditation One

CHANGING BELIEFS ABOUT CANCER

After you are comfortably settled, take in slow, deep breaths, and as you breathe out, mentally say to yourself, "Relax." Pay attention to your breathing and continue to repeat "Relax" as you exhale. When you feel ready, close your eyes . . .

As you continue to breathe deeply, slowly, and comfortably, begin to notice any tension in your head and your scalp, and as you exhale, let your head and scalp relax. Breathe in, breathe out, and mentally say to yourself, "Relax." . . . Notice any tension in your jaw, and let your jaw relax . . .

Breathe deeply, slowly, and comfortably, and continue to let your body relax. Let your neck and your shoulders relax . . . and your arms and your hands . . .

And now let your back relax . . . and then your chest . . . and then your abdomen . . . and then your pelvis. This allows your heart and your lungs and your stomach—all your organs—to relax. Breathe deeply, slowly, and comfortably . . . and relax.

Continue downward and let your hips relax . . . and your legs . . . and your feet . . .

And now with your body more relaxed, begin to imagine yourself in a place where you feel safe, comfortable, and protected. The place can be real or imagined, a place you've been to or a place you've never seen before. Take a moment to imagine this place as you continue to breathe slowly, deeply, and comfortably.

And now focus your thoughts on your body . . . Imagine your body as strong and wise, your white blood cells as strong and numerous and very capable of taking care of you . . . Breathe in deeply . . . exhale . . . relax . . . Remember that, of itself, cancer is composed of weak, deformed cells easily eliminated from your body . . .

Imagine your treatment as being helpful . . . imagine your treatment as a friend helping you to get well . . . You might imagine your treatment weakening the cancer cells or strengthening and increasing the white cells (whatever you understand is the action of your treatment) . . . Your treatment is acting appropriately for your situation.

Now imagine yourself excited and enthusiastic about your treatment . . . Imagine that your body is cooperating with your chosen treatment to heal itself . . .

And imagine that your cancer is a messenger, communicating a message sent from a loving source to you, making you aware of the ways that you need to change to become more of who you are . . . moving you away from pain and toward joy and peace . . . Imagine that your cancer has brought this message from a loving source . . .

And now imagine one step you can take to act on this message to change . . . one step you can take to become more of who you are . . . or one step you can take to help you experience less pain in your life . . .

Commit to taking that action and decide on what date you will take the first step . . .

And imagine what it will feel like as you begin to regain your natural state of health . . . Your white blood cells are increasing and removing the cancer cells from your body with ease . . . the cancer can subside now; it is leaving your body, having served as a messenger that brought about needed changes in your life . . .

Now become aware of your breathing again . . . Focus on being conscious of the room again . . . returning to your *normal waking consciousness with a sense of calm and peace.*

Immediately after you complete this meditation exercise, write down what action you are going to take to bring yourself more joy in life and less pain. Commit to that action by also writing down when you're going to take the first step. Remember, it's better to start with a small step right away than to wait until later to take a bigger one.

Our inner wisdom doesn't always give us answers right away. If no answer has come to you, create an answer from your conscious mind. As you act on that answer, stay open to guidance from a deeper level. It may emerge during meditation or at any time during the following days. When an answer does come, write it down and act on it.

As you continue to work with this meditation, you will be learning healthier beliefs about cancer, which will then develop into a healthier unconscious attitude. You can evaluate your own learning progress quite easily. Become aware of your automatic emotional response when you hear cancer discussed now (on the news, in newspapers, in magazines, at the doctor's office, around the hospital, in your support group). Then compare what your automatic emotional response is after a few weeks of work.

Remember to pay attention to your energy levels and adjust your imagery practice to your needs. The goal in this or any other meditation work is to enrich your life and your health through conscious, intentional thinking.

If you become frustrated by your meditation work, give some thought to where that frustration comes from. Are you creating images that are so complex that you can't recall them? Keep the images simple. Do you need more information about how your treatment works in order to imagine it defeating the cancer or strengthening your immune system?

I often ask patients to explain to me what their treatment does, so that we can clarify any misunderstandings and they can approach it with confidence. If they are taking chemotherapy, we work on clarifying their image of the cancer cells under attack. The cancer cells are weak and confused and vulnerable, an easy target for the medicine, while the normal cells are much stronger and able to resist its toxic effect.

Our patients imagine the entire treatment in detail, as if they could see inside their bodies and watch individual cells in action. Often they see the chemotherapy drug as little tiny pills or little drops of liquid moving quickly through the body, where the cancer cells ingest the drug. Some patients imagine the cancer cells exploding and healthy cells coming to clean up the debris. Others see the cancer cells getting weaker and weaker until they die. Other patients imagine they themselves are white blood cells moving through the bloodstream, directing other white blood cells, and destroying cancer cells. We also put a lot of emphasis on the intelligence of the normal cells, who realize the drug is not for them. This helps to reduce side effects. If the patient is considering surgery, we work on imagining the surgeon and operating room team as calm and confident, the operation going smoothly, the cancer removed, the body healing promptly. Ask for whatever information you need to imagine the best possible outcome of your treatment.

The images that work for you may change over time. Honor this. The essential elements are imagining the cancer as weak, the body as strong, and the treatment as effective.

Once they have developed images that feel right for

them, many patients record them as part of this meditation. They often take the tapes with them when they are receiving treatment. This can help to relax you, cut out distractions, and enhance the effect of the treatment itself.

Do you believe that the meditation takes too long and is too taxing? Do it less often or break it up into segments. For example, you could work on imagining treatment as a friend during one meditation, and then picture cancer as a messenger during another meditation. When you feel comfortable with both images, combine them into one meditation again.

It is extremely important to do this work at your own pace. If you continue to feel that your energy level is lower after meditation, then get help from someone experienced in counseling people with cancer. Meditation is intended to enhance your sense of well-being and increase your energy level.

I suggest you take a break from your work at this point and start the next section tomorrow or after you have rested.

USING IMAGERY AND MEDITATION TO DEVELOP TRUST AND INNER WISDOM

The workings of the imagination can be divided into mental processes and spiritual processes. Thoughts, memories, ideas, learning, mental rehearsal, and desensitization (going over something again and again in your mind in order to lessen its impact on your emotions) could all be considered mental processes. Intuition, gut feelings, hunches, answers to prayers, and messages received in meditation could all be considered spiritual processes.

You can use both the mental and spiritual aspects of the imagination in your meditations, intentionally creating mental images and intentionally being receptive to spiritual images.

Many of my patients ask: How do I tell the difference between a conversation going on in my head and a truly inspirational message from spirit? I find that, first of all, an inspirational message comes with a feeling of rightness. For example, let's say I had cancer and in meditation I asked, "Will I die from cancer?" If I first hear "yes" and then I hear "no," and then I argue with myself about what could happen, what should happen, and what happened in the past, I would say that this was clearly not a spiritual message.

If, on the other hand, I asked the same question in meditation and then felt a strong sense of knowing, with the thought "I am alive right this moment," I would accept and use this answer as guidance. To me, this answer would mean that my question about dying from cancer is irrelevant, and that it is important to focus on the fact that I am alive today. I would act on that message. I would ask myself, "What can I do in the present to honor my being alive right now?"

In the first meditation, the focus was on mental processes—you imagined your body, the cancer, and the treatment. Toward the end of the meditation, the focus broadened and you began to bring spiritual processes into your imagination—you considered that cancer could be a messenger from a loving source. In the next meditation, you will go more deeply into spiritual processes, further exploring your beliefs about the nature of cancer.

As you did with the previous meditation, you may want to tape this or have someone else tape it or read it aloud to you.

Meditation Two

DEVELOPING TRUST

After you are comfortably settled, take in slow, deep breaths, and as you breathe out, mentally say to yourself, "Relax." Pay attention to your breathing and continue to repeat "Relax" as you exhale. When you feel ready, close your eyes . . .

As you continue to breathe deeply, slowly, and comfortably, begin to notice any tension in your head and your scalp, and as you exhale, let your head and scalp relax. Breathe in, breathe out, and mentally say to yourself, "Relax." . . . Notice any tension in your jaw, and let your jaw relax . . .

Breathe deeply, slowly, and comfortably, and continue to let your body relax. Let your neck and your shoulders relax . . . and your arms and your hands.

Now let your back relax . . . and then your chest . . . and then your abdomen . . . and then your pelvis. This allows your heart and your lungs and your stomach—all your organs—to relax. Breathe deeply, slowly, and comfortably and relax . . .

Continue downward and let your hips relax . . . and your legs . . . and your feet . . .

And now with your body more relaxed, begin to imagine yourself in a place where you feel safe, comfortable, and protected. The place can be real or imagined, a place you've been to or a place you've never seen before. Take a moment to imagine this place as you continue to breathe slowly, deeply, and comfortably . . .

When you are ready, begin to imagine that you have been born into a world where you are intended to be happy, healthy, and deeply fulfilled . . . Imagine that you have within you a genetic blueprint intended to be lived out over a long, full lifetime . . . When those pieces of the pattern are completed after a full life, you will feel a deep sense of completion. Imagine how that pattern is communicated to you throughout your life . . . through quiet, subtle messages, things that go by the name of instinct, intuition, gut feeling, inner wisdom . . .

Imagine the direction of your path being reinforced by the entire world, the entire universe . . . reinforced by harmony, joy, and fulfillment . . .

Now imagine how it has been for you since you were born . . . Remember the loud messages that came into your life, saying, "Do this" and "Don't do that." . . . Remember the voices that said, "Do this if you want to be loved," or "Don't do that if you want to be loved." . . . "Be this!" And, "Don't be that!" . . . "Do this!" and "Don't do that!"

And imagine how those loud voices drowned out the soft, subtle voices of your excitement, your dreams and imaginings, and remember how you, like everyone else, followed the loud voices . . . Imagine how the entire world, the entire universe has tried to bring you back, sometimes using frustration, pain, or illness to keep you from going farther away from who you are . . .

And now imagine that you understand more of what is going on and has been going on in your life . . . And imagine that you are paying more attention to those things that make you feel good and those things that make you feel bad, recognizing them as signals to continue or to stop . . . Commit to honoring those feelings when you recognize them . . . Honor the messages coming in from the whole world; honor the belief that the whole universe wants you to be who you are and will help you be who you are . . .

*And now imagine yourself becoming still and quiet . . .
listening to instinct, intuition, gut feeling, inner wisdom
. . . listening to an inner wisdom that leads you in the
direction of more joy and deep fulfillment . . . and less
pain, frustration, and illness.*

*Imagine that the entire world, the entire universe,
rejoices because your joy is felt everywhere and your harmony adds to the harmony of the whole world, the whole
universe . . .*

*And now imagine that as you open your eyes, you are
returning to the room with a sense of that joy and harmony
. . . And slowly begin to become aware of where you are,
and the light and the noises of the room . . . And when
you are ready, open your eyes and return to your waking
consciousness with a sense of calm and peace.*

This is a way to begin developing more trust or confidence in yourself, your world, and your universe. You are
deepening your relationship with yourself, your world, your
universe, with all that there is. In this meditation, you
assumed the posture of believing that the creative forces in
and around us are good and here to help us, knowing what
is best for us and giving us what we need out of love and
understanding. We will work further with these concepts in
the letter series.

This meditation work may require much energy and be
followed by many deep thoughts. Please consider stopping
your work for today and continue tomorrow or sometime
after that, whenever you feel ready. For now, I recommend
that you do something fun, joyful, or peaceful, or take part
in some other nurturing activity.

WORKING WITH YOUR INNER WISDOM

In the first meditation, you considered that cancer might be bringing you a message. In the second meditation, you began to develop the possibility that this messenger comes from a source that is trying to direct you toward health and a more joyful life. Now we are going to go one step further, again moving more deeply into spiritual processes, by trying to clearly connect with your inner wisdom.

Meditation Three

COMMUNICATING WITH YOUR INNER WISDOM

After you are comfortably settled, take in slow, deep breaths, and as you breathe out, mentally say to yourself, "Relax." Pay attention to your breathing and continue to repeat "Relax" as you exhale. When you feel ready, close your eyes . . .

As you continue to breathe deeply, slowly, and comfortably, begin to notice any tension in your head and your scalp and, as you exhale, let your head and scalp relax. Notice any tension in your jaw, and let your jaw relax . . .

Breathe deeply, slowly, and comfortably, and continue to let your body relax. Let your neck and your shoulders relax . . . and your arms and your hands . . .

And now let your back relax . . . and then your chest . . . and then your abdomen . . and then your pelvis. This lets your heart and your lungs and your stomach—all your organs—relax. Breathe deeply, slowly, and comfortably and relax . . .

Continue moving your attention downward . . . and let your hips relax . . . and your legs . . . and your feet . . .

Now, with your body more relaxed, begin to picture yourself in a place where you feel safe, comfortable, and protected. The place can be real or imagined, a place you've been to or a place you've never seen before. Take a moment to imagine this place as you continue to breathe slowly, deeply, and comfortably . . .

As you relax in this special place, in your own way, in your own time, begin to call upon your inner wisdom, asking for help and guidance . . . Imagine that your inner wisdom is listening and responding to your request for help . . . Let your inner wisdom take any form you like . . . It could be a person you know who has died . . . It could be a spiritual figure, a religious figure . . . It might be an old person . . . or a young person . . . an animal . . . an indistinguishable form . . . or a light.

Or your inner wisdom may manifest as a thought . . . or a still, quiet voice . . . or only a feeling or sense of something being present. Take your time and let your inner wisdom come to you in a way that you can hear it and communicate with it . . .

Allow yourself to see, hear, or sense your inner wisdom, knowing that it brings a message of love from the universe . . .

If you are not comfortable with the first form that presents itself, move on to another form . . . You will know when you have connected with the messenger by the way you feel—a feeling of rightness . . .

When you are ready, ask whatever questions you have . . . What do you need to do to get well? What do you need to do to take care of yourself? What do you need to begin to change? . . . No question is inappropriate . . . What do you need to know?

When an answer comes, does the answer feel right? If not, continue to ask the question . . . Know that the true answers come with feeling . . . the answers come with the feeling, "Ah yes, I know that's right." The answers come with insight . . .

And when you have an answer, agree to take action. Decide what step you will take to initiate this action . . . When will you take this step? On what specific date?

If no answers come, or no answers come with a definite feeling that they are the right answers, then create your own answer. Decide on an action you could take to acknowledge your answer. And commit to that action. Decide what your first step will be . . . and when.

Resolve to act on your decisions as soon as you reasonably can, knowing that your actions will bring more joy into your life and into the lives of others . . . Resolve to do the things that make sense for you to do . . . and decide now how you will initiate the action and when you will take that first step.

Sometimes you will not get answers to your questions. When that happens, create your own answer and act on the answer you created . . . And while you are acting on your answer, acknowledge that you didn't get the answer you wanted, and that you are open to receiving one when it comes . . .

Take a moment to appreciate yourself for taking the time and energy to communicate with your inner wisdom . . . And when you are ready, become aware of your breathing again . . . Focus on being conscious of the room again, returning to your normal waking consciousness with a sense of calm and peace.

Patients often receive messages from a family member who has died, or from a religious or spiritual figure. Many experience a message coming from light rather than from a person. The light is most often white, gold, or blue. Some patients tell me that their inner wisdom manifests in very imaginative ways, from transparent green forms to family pets! It really doesn't matter what type of form appears to you, as long as you feel comfortable with it.

It's also okay if you don't imagine your inner wisdom appearing to you in any visual form. When we focused on inner wisdom taking the form of a guide, we found that many of our patients had difficulty with the meditation. When we broadened the concept to let the inner wisdom manifest in a thought or voice or feeling, patients began to use the process more easily. I think you will find it productive to keep doing this meditation, so that your inner wisdom can contribute to all your work with this book.

You could use your inner wisdom to check out what you really need right now in terms of support, for example. If you are a support person, you can use your inner wisdom to determine what you need and how to communicate that to the person with cancer. In your meditations, ask your inner wisdom about anything that concerns you right now.

When I first began studying imagery and meditation, I attended a motivational sales seminar where we did a meditation similar to the one you just learned, only in this case we were to meet what were called "advisers." (This kept the focus on business.) We were told to picture an elevator that would go up or down. When the doors opened, the adviser would be revealed. If you didn't like the adviser, you could put him or her back on the elevator and send for another one.

In doing this exercise, the first time I saw an adviser, she was a young businesswoman wearing a suit. As directed in the exercise, I asked her what her name was. She told me I was not ready to know. I asked why, and she told me I just wasn't ready. On the second try, I saw this businesswoman again, and again I asked her for her name and she told me I wasn't ready. So I asked her what I needed to do to get ready. She said I had to take the process more seriously.

Later in the day when we did the exercise for the third time, I saw the same woman, and this time she told me her name was Mary. I said, "Oh, Mary! As in Mary, Mary quite contrary?" In a very stern tone, she replied, "No. I am Mary." When she said this, I had an experience unlike any I had ever had in my life. All of a sudden, I knew this was the Biblical Mary. I say "knew" because it came with such deep feeling; I had something far beyond an intellectual understanding. A flood of emotion swept over me, as I began to see a vision of the world and the universe.

The vision itself is difficult to describe, but from it, I could see that everything on this earth is good—everything and everyone is meant to exist. I understood that this goodness had little to do with what we were all acting out or with how the human race was behaving. I could see and feel that we are all made of the same substance as God. There was great calm in knowing this, and the knowing was at a different level than anything I had ever experienced. I began to sob deeply from a place of great joy. I had an understanding of the pain I had gone through in life, as well as the pain of life in general. It was a wonderful experience. I was in a state of ecstasy for hours. Although the visualization itself lasted less than five minutes, it significantly changed my life.

Was this truly the Biblical Mary who appeared to me? I don't think that matters. Whether it was Mary or a visual metaphor for Mary, I felt it was she, and I have continued to call on her regularly throughout the years for help and guidance—as well as on other forms of inner wisdom.

Reid worked with the inner wisdom meditation only a short time before he decided that the inner wisdom he was seeking was God. To Reid, the inner wisdom comes from Spirit, which guides him in whatever information or assistance he is seeking. For him, working with inner wisdom is really prayer and meditation, talking to God and listening.

Please consider stopping your reading for today and approach the next section tomorrow or whenever you feel ready.

WORKING WITH PAIN

I have found that patients most often doubt their ability to influence their health during times of pain. But it is possible to use pain as an opportunity to strengthen your influence over your body. At the center, we do a good deal of work on the mental and emotional aspects of pain, and we find a huge variation in results. Some people experience a reversal of painful symptoms. Others are able to lessen their pain medication. Meditation is a tool to use against pain, just as medication is. For some, it is a marvelous answer, for others, only a small part of the answer.

My philosophy has always been that you should have the pain relief you need. Being in pain is very counterproductive. It is a huge drain on your energy, and it takes away your ability to attend to anything else in life. I have never failed to prescribe pain medication if it is needed to keep a patient comfortable, and I have never encountered a problem with addiction unless the patient was addicted to begin with. Use the amount of medication you need as feedback about other aspects of your mental and emotional state.

At our center, we help our patients to look at pain as a message of love, just as we look at the illness itself. Don't ignore your pain or try to tough it out. Instead, ask yourself, "How is my pain trying to help me?" Pain always has two components: the underlying physical condition, and the message it is trying to give you. Do what you need to in order to alleviate the physical pain, but do the mental and emotional work as well. The mental–emotional element of pain may be large or small, but it is always there.

Here's a practical experiment: The next time you feel pain of any kind, assume that the pain serves the purpose of distracting you from a difficult challenge in your life. Ask yourself, "If I were not experiencing this pain, what would I be thinking about?" Ask this repeatedly. My experience is that answers come after asking three or four times. When the problem is dealt with in healthy ways (generally by changing unhealthy beliefs to healthier ones), often the pain goes away. The following meditation will help you deal with pain in this way.

Some patients fear that paying attention to their pain will only increase it. After twenty-five years of working with pain, I'm a pragmatist. If distraction works for you, if you can make your pain go away for a while by listening to music or seeing a movie, that's fine. But most of us are so afraid of pain and resist it so fiercely that allowing ourselves to come closer to our pain may actually lessen it. The following meditation helps you use your imagination to create a more intimate relationship with your pain, so that you can begin to listen to it more comfortably and influence it more directly.

Before you meditate, write down in your journal what your pain is protecting you from. Then write down your beliefs about that subject. On another page, write down healthier beliefs. When you are ready to begin, keep the list of healthier beliefs close at hand so you can open your eyes and look at it.

Meditation Four

INCREASING YOUR TRUST IN YOURSELF THROUGH WORKING WITH PAIN

After you are comfortably settled, take in slow, deep breaths, and as you breathe out, mentally say to yourself, "Relax." Pay attention to your breathing and continue to repeat "Relax" as you exhale. When you feel ready, close your eyes . . .

As you continue to breathe deeply, slowly, and comfortably, begin to notice any tension in your head and your scalp and, as you exhale, let your head and scalp relax. Notice any tension in your jaw, and let your jaw relax . . .

Breathe deeply, slowly, and comfortably, and continue to let your body relax. Let your neck and your shoulders relax . . . and your arms and your hands . . .

And now let your back relax . . . and then your chest . . . and then your abdomen . . . and then your pelvis. This allows your heart and your lungs and your stomach— all your organs—to relax. Breathe deeply, slowly, and comfortably and relax . . .

Continue downward and let your hips relax . . . and your legs . . . and your feet . . .

And now with your body more relaxed, begin to imagine yourself in a place where you are safe, comfortable, and protected . . . Take a moment to imagine this place of great safety and comfort as you continue to breathe slowly, deeply, and comfortably . . .

When you feel ready, begin to focus on the area of pain and relax this area . . . Breathe in, breathe out, and relax the area of pain . . . Picture the area as a tight rubber band and hold this image for a couple of seconds . . . Now let the rubber band go limp; let the area of pain relax . . .

Do this again . . . Consciously tighten the area of pain for a couple of seconds and then relax . . . relax the area of pain.

As the area relaxes, send gold light into it . . . imagine gold light going into the area of pain . . .

And as the area relaxes, feel blood flowing to it . . . feel energy flowing to it . . . Relax the area and make room for the blood and energy to flow into it . . .

Breathing slowly, deeply, and comfortably, begin to imagine the color of your pain. What color is your pain? . . . Change the color to whatever color you like . . . Picture the color more intense . . . and then less intense.

Continue to breathe slowly, deeply, and comfortably and now begin to imagine the texture of your pain . . . Is it rough? . . . Is it smooth? . . . Is the pain hard . . . or soft? Change the texture to whatever you would like . . .

Make your image of the pain larger . . . and smaller . . .

And now as you continue to breathe slowly, deeply, and comfortably, send your breath into the area of pain . . . Imagine that your breath brings light into the area . . . Imagine a gold light flowing into the area of pain . . .

Calling on your inner wisdom for strength and support, recall the difficult life circumstances or unhealthy beliefs this pain is protecting you from . . . When you are ready, open your eyes for a moment and read the new beliefs that you would like to hold . . . Take your time. Mentally repeat *them to yourself, then close your eyes again and relax . . . Breathe slowly, deeply, and comfortably . . .*

Now imagine yourself doing whatever is important for you to do to take care of a difficult challenge in your life . . . What is the first step toward meeting that challenge? When will you initiate this action? How?

And now imagine what your life will be like after this difficulty has gone away . . . Imagine how your life will improve, how your relationship with yourself and with others will improve . . .

And now imagine that the painful area is becoming normal again . . . Imagine you are pain-free . . . You feel good, you feel strong . . .

And when you are ready, become aware of your breathing again and aware of the sounds in the room . . . Slowly open your eyes, returning to your normal waking consciousness with a sense of calm and peace . . .

Use this meditation regularly three to four times per day for ten to fifteen minutes.

Here is another technique I have found useful, especially when you don't have time or desire to do an entire meditation. When your pain occurs, imagine yourself involved in some healthful activity—ask your inner wisdom for help in what healthful activity to imagine.

For example, I once had a major problem with an acutely arthritic ankle. I discovered that the beliefs I needed to change revolved around work and support in my work. The image I needed to hold was of playing ball with my children. I called up the image before I started to walk, and it then seemed that the activity was preparing my ankle to be strong and flexible enough to play with my children. The image gave a larger purpose to my pain. Instead of just having to walk across the room to answer the telephone, I was doing a rehabilitation exercise. The discomfort was still there, but I could relax into it, rather than pulling away and bracing myself to resist it. It was a different experience, and far less painful.

I'd like to describe for you how this process worked for one man who came to our center in severe pain from advanced cancer. He was taking so much medication that he felt drowsy all the time, and he was wearing himself out by constant activity because his pain bothered him more when he was still. We also discovered that he was deeply worried about the manufacturing company he headed. His list of beliefs looked like this:

I'm going to go bankrupt and lose my business.
I will lose my home and won't be able to provide for my family.
My wife will leave me, and I'm going to be all alone.
So I'm going to die miserably broke and all alone.

Using the five questions to evaluate these beliefs, he developed new, incompatible beliefs to use in meditation:

I may or may not need to declare bankruptcy, and even if I do, there is much I can do to take care of myself financially.
I may or may not decide to move to a less expensive home. My family may need to change their lifestyle, and that can be done in ways that are good for all of us.
My wife may or may not leave me, and there are still other very important people in my life.
I am going to die eventually, but I don't have to be broke, and I certainly don't have to be alone, and there is much I can do to influence these things.

As often as his pain came up as a reminder, he focused on these healthier beliefs. He also shared them with his wife, and their relationship started to shift dramatically. She assured him that she had no intention of leaving him for financial or health reasons, and she helped him to think through their financial alternatives.

As his pain waxed and waned, he began to observe a clear relationship between what he was thinking and how much pain he was feeling. He also began to imagine himself playing golf again, and he found he could decrease his pain in walking by thinking about strengthening himself for golf. Gradually, he cut back on his pain medication because he found he needed less, not because he thought he ought to. He also realized that his pain was worse the first thing in the morning. We suggested that he set his alarm for an hour before he wanted to get up, so that he could take his medication then and later get out of bed feeling good. For him, not getting up to pain in the morning made a difference all day long.

As you can see, there was no one solution that worked for this man. It was his own willingness to explore his pain and to use the tools we gave him that enabled him to dramatically improve his sense of well-being.

The last meditation in this chapter focuses on lessening the fear of death. If you decide not to go on to this section, that's perfectly acceptable. Do it when you feel ready. At this point, if you've worked with the first four meditations, you've already made progress toward holding healthy beliefs about yourself and the nature of your universe. Keep working with these meditations according to your own needs and desires. Continue to pay close attention to your energy level following meditation, and adjust the time you spend with this work accordingly.

USING MEDITATION TO DECREASE THE FEAR OF DEATH

I believe it is of great benefit to use the process of meditation to begin to deal with one of the greatest obstacles of life: facing the fear of death. If you are not ready to do this work, skip it. Come back to it when you are ready. That could be days from now, weeks from now, months from now, even years from now. You can still proceed with the work in this book. Simply move on to Chapter 5, The Two-Year Health Plan, instead.

Death is one of the most delicate and explosive topics we address during the Simonton Cancer Center's new patient program. A small but significant number of people become depressed when this topic is introduced. Confronting and working through that depression takes a good deal of time and energy. Therefore, I suggest you get inner guidance. Quiet yourself and ask your inner wisdom if this is a good time for you to explore death. If the answer is yes, and if that answer comes with a strong feeling that it's okay for you to do this now, then feel free to continue with this section. If the answer is no, or you feel uncertain, once again I suggest you go on to the next section. Come back to this one when you feel it is right for you to do so. If you are working with a therapist, you would certainly want to get him or her to help you with your work around death.

The purpose of exploring death is to decrease your fear of death, and in so doing, increase your energy for living life today. You can do this by shifting your less healthy beliefs about death and dying to healthier beliefs about death and dying, using imagery to help you make these changes, just as you did with the meditation about cancer and treatment.

It may be helpful to remind yourself that our predominant cultural beliefs about death are quite unhealthy. In our culture, dying is believed to be a long, painful experience over which we have no significant influence; death is a sign of failure; death is the worst thing that can happen to us. Try testing the relative health value of these beliefs with the five questions listed on page 67. Also consider that our primary cultural tool for dealing with death is denial. Most of us deal with death by pretending that death doesn't exist, and we do this in the face of 200,000 people dying on our planet daily. I want you to take a moment to appreciate the fact that you are moving away from these unhealthy cultural beliefs and out of denial just by reading this section of the book.

In looking at your own beliefs about death and dying, three areas are important to examine:

1. Your beliefs about death and dying in general
2. Your beliefs about what your own dying process will be
3. Your beliefs about life after death.

Use the first four questions on page 67 (Many people skip the fifth question, as they consider the "facts" about life after death unknowable, or at least debatable.) to determine the health value of your beliefs.

Much has been learned in the past twenty to thirty years from Elisabeth Kübler-Ross, Raymond Moody, and others doing very important work in the area of death and dying. Drawing on their experience, I will give you some generally healthy beliefs to consider:

1. You can influence your dying in much the same way that you can influence your living. If you want to die a certain way, then it is important to live that way.

2. Death is a brief transition period between physical life as we know it and an existence that comes afterward.

Death is the end of this physical existence, just as birth was the beginning.

3. After death, your essence, or your soul, continues on in an existence that is desirable.

To aid you in shifting your beliefs toward these or other healthy beliefs about death and dying, I am going to give you the meditation that we use in our patient sessions. If your support person is participating in the exercises with you and also feels ready to do this process, the two of you may find this meditation a helpful way to discuss the fears that both of you may be experiencing. Just getting these thoughts out into the open can help strengthen the channels of communication between you.

Meditation Five

Increasing Your Energy for Getting Well by Decreasing the Fear of Death

After you are comfortably settled, take in slow, deep breaths, and as you breathe out, mentally say to yourself, "Relax." Pay attention to your breathing and continue to repeat "Relax" as you exhale. When you feel ready, close your eyes . . .

As you continue to breathe deeply, slowly, and comfortably, begin to notice any tension in your head and your scalp and, as you exhale, let your head and scalp relax. Breathe in, breathe out, and mentally say to yourself, "Relax." . . . Notice any tension in your jaw, and let your jaw relax . . .

Breathe deeply, slowly, and comfortably, and now continue to let your body relax. Let your neck and your shoulders relax . . . and your arms and your hands . . .

Now let your back relax . . . and then your chest . . . and then your abdomen . . . and then your pelvis. This allows your heart and your lungs and your stomach—all your organs—to relax. Breathe deeply, slowly, and comfortably and relax . . .

Continue moving your attention down your body and let your hips relax . . . and your legs . . . and your feet . . .

And now with your body more relaxed, continue to breathe deeply, slowly, and comfortably. When you are

ready, begin to imagine yourself approaching death . . .
Where are you? How old do you appear to be?

Imagine yourself in whatever surroundings you would
like to be when death comes . . . Imagine yourself at the
age you would like to be when death comes . . .

Now continue to imagine yourself moving closer and
closer to death . . . Imagine yourself on your death bed . . .
Who is there? What is being said?

Breathe deeply and relax . . . relax . . . Imagine yourself on your death bed . . . Imagine yourself surrounded by
those you want to be with you . . . And imagine yourself
exchanging messages of love and being comforted by those
who are with you . . . What do you need to say? What do
you need to do to be ready to let go? . . . Whatever those
things are, know that you need to say them and do them
now . . .

Continue to imagine yourself moving closer and closer
to death . . . Now you are beginning the actual process of
dying . . . Your energy, your essence, your soul is beginning
to leave your physical body . . .

Feel the energy moving up from your feet. Cooperate
with that energy, allowing it to move upward through your
body, feeling it move out the top of your head . . . You are
moving toward the light . . . always toward the light . . .
You are moving in harmony with the loving and creative
forces of the universe . . . Focus on images that make you
feel good . . . Imagine yourself in the flow of the universe
. . . Breathe deeply . . . Follow your breath.

The universe is breathing you, taking care of you . . .
You are leaving the body and going toward the light . . .
You are joining the loving, creative forces that created all of
us . . . And you can relax . . . relax . . .

As you join with the creative forces of the universe, you
now have a new perspective. You can look back over your

life . . . What would you have done more often? What would you have done less often?

Decide to start doing more of the things that bring you joy and less of the things that give you pain. What are you going to do to bring more joy into your life? What will be your first step toward that goal?

And now, feeling free from the physical body, you can begin to explore . . . Imagine yourself getting ready to be born . . . Where will you be? Who would you like to be? What would be important to you in your new life?

As you begin to make new choices and experience change, you are dying to the old and being born to the new . . . You are dying to the old experiences and the old beliefs and being born to new experiences and new beliefs . . . Know that this process goes on and on . . . that you are constantly dying to the old and being born to the new . . . You are always letting go of one moment to move to the next . . .

And now, as you prepare to return to your normal waking consciousness, remember the thoughts and the feelings of comfort that you would like to bring back with you . . . Remember the decisions that you made about any changes you want to make in your life, as well as what you will do to initiate those changes and when you will take that first step . . . Remember that you are considering new beliefs about death and dying that will give you more energy and enthusiasm for living life today . . . And bring these thoughts back with you now as you return . . .

When you are ready, begin to be aware of your breathing again . . . become aware of the light in the room . . . and be aware of the noises around you . . . When you are ready, open your eyes.

My experience with this process has been that it is almost universally uplifting and energizing for those people who feel ready to participate in it. If you found the process difficult, please get help from your therapist, or discuss your feelings in your support group or with those you consider to be part of your support system. Now is a good time to practice asking for any help that you need.

Whether or not you have actually participated in the meditation on death or simply read through this section, please consider stopping your reading for today.

5

The Two-Year Health Plan

Setting Goals for Getting Well

I hope I have conveyed that work with mental and spiritual processes is of the utmost importance. However, just working with mental and spiritual processes would put one out of balance; it is also essential to stay grounded in the physical world. Developing a two-year health plan involves some deep thinking, but it is basically about changing your day-to-day routines in six areas over the next two years. If you were only to think about what you wanted to do and meditate on those things, you still might get little done. However, the two-year health plan will help you translate your intentions into physical realities.

As a businessman who was accustomed to using plans, charts, and graphs in his work, Reid really took to creating and using his two-year health plan. Even when you feel ill, setting and meeting your goals will give you a real sense of accomplishment and progress towards health.

The goals to set in your two-year health plan are bottom line goals, the minimum you intend to accomplish. Don't be in a hurry to create a plan for yourself. Set goals with the attitude that *this is what you are going to do,* not what you want to do or might do. Take time to examine your beliefs about each area and check those beliefs against Maultsby's five questions (Chapter 4, page 67) for their relative health value. This week, do no more than setting your goals in the first three areas. Take several weeks to complete your work on this assignment. You can continue to come back to it as you work on the letter series. Of course, you are always free to change whatever plan you create, since it is simply a framework on which to build.

Please refer to the sample on the facing page to help you follow the instructions. At the end of the chapter, we have provided a blank chart that you may want to copy so that you can make several drafts before you settle on your plan.

CREATING YOUR PLAN

Step One

Life activities have been artificially divided into six different categories: purpose in life, play, exercise, social support, nutrition, and creative thinking. To begin this exercise, carefully read the following explanation of the six categories:

1. *Purpose in life:* Activities that answer the question, "Why am I here?" These might include your occupation, your role in the family, your spiritual or civic activities, or anything else that gives you a reason or zest for living.

2. *Play:* Any activity that produces the feeling of joy or that can be considered as "having fun."

TWO-YEAR PERSONAL HEALTH PLAN

	3 months	6 months	9 months	12 months	15 months	18 months	21 months	24 months
Nutrition	4 healthy meals per week	6 healthy meals per week	8 healthy meals per week					14 healthy meals per week
Social Support		1 hour per week	2 hours per week					6 hours per week
Play			30 minutes per week					7 hours per week
Purpose								5 hours per week
Meditation								20 minutes a day, 6 days each week
Exercise								15 minutes, 3 days each week

STOP HERE FOR NOW
FINISH THE PLAN OVER
THE NEXT SEVERAL WEEKS

3. *Exercise:* Any physical activity or any time spent mentally focusing on physical activities (especially for those temporarily unable to exercise).

4. *Social support:* The time you spend with family and friends, or time you spend with a psychotherapist, minister, church group, or support group.

5. *Nutrition:* This category includes not just eating, but any efforts you make around food and nutrition—preparing meals, taking vitamins, going to support groups that focus on diet, and reading or educating yourself about food and nutrition. Your beliefs about food and nutrition are vitally important.

6. *Creative thinking:* Meditation and imagery are included in this category, as are any specific forms of intentional relaxation. Reading, seminars, or courses related to these areas can also be included.

Step Two

On a sheet of paper, write down each category, then list the activities you do that fall into each category. (Remember that in real life, several categories may run together in one activity. Classify that activity as you wish; there are no right or wrong answers.) Estimate the number of hours you spend each week in each area. You will probably be surprised at some of your answers. Does your time allotment reflect a balanced approach to life? Does it reflect the values you like to believe you hold? Does it reflect your true priorities?

Many patients realize that they are spending 90 percent of their time on things they think they should do and only 10 percent on things they want to do. They need a better balance between their obligations and their desires. An overbalance in the "should" direction can lead to depression and hopelessness, while our desires will naturally move us in the direction of balance.

Looking ahead two years, what would you like most to change? You don't have to be precise at this point, but setting some general long-term directions is important.

Step Three

Rank the order of the categories as based on your desire to work on them, plus your experience with them. For example, if you spend most of your energy on social support but you would really like to spend more time on diet and nutrition, then diet and nutrition might be your first priority.

On the other hand, if you have never paid attention to nutrition and are strictly an "eat to live" type, don't put this category first just because you think you should. Make your first priority something you are already interested in or know you will enjoy.

Enter your categories in order on a chart like that shown on page 107. (A blank chart is provided at the end of the chapter.)

Step Four

Now you will begin to set more specific goals. For the first category, your number one priority, you will create a three-month goal. I recommend to our patients that this goal be *half* of whatever they are currently doing in that category. For example, if you chose to focus on nutrition first, and you are now eating eight healthy meals a week, for your three-month goal, write down four healthy meals a week. Remember: This is not an upper limit, it is a lower limit—you want to do this much, regardless of circumstances. You would have to try to fail in order not to meet this goal.

After the three-month goal, create the six-month and the nine-month goals, again for the first category only. If the three-month goal is four healthy meals, the six-month goal might be six healthy meals, and the nine-month goal might be eight healthy meals—the point where you are now.

On the surface, setting goals this way may seem counterproductive, so let me explain why this approach works. You're not using these goals to limit yourself, you are simply setting bottom line goals. You will almost automatically do more than what you write down as your goal. You also need to keep in mind that because you have an illness and are undergoing treatment, you may want to do a little less than you have in the recent past. Bottom line goals give you flexibility. They also help you appreciate what you are currently doing.

This method of setting goals also confronts fear-producing thoughts like, "I've got to hurry up and make some changes or I am going to die." Setting a gentle pace helps you deal with that kind of desperation and fear in a healthy way. This method also stops you from taking something you may never have done, such as exercise, and making it your first priority with unreasonable goals. This doesn't mean that you can't exercise at all; it means you move gently into exercise. You can go ahead and exercise in any way you believe is appropriate; however, your focus is on the long term—the level you want to achieve two years from now and how to get there in a healthy way. You don't have to put pressure on yourself to get there tomorrow.

Going more slowly also allows you to fulfill your goals in a pleasureable way. You don't want to create more "shoulds" for yourself! Use your creativity to make healthy changes fun or exciting. Try to move them into the "desire" category. Don't take up jogging if you dislike it, even if someone tells you it is excellent exercise. Find something you enjoy—however it may be rated by fitness experts—so that you feel you are rewarding yourself when you take time for exercise.

Finally, be aware of a crucial category not listed here: rest. Pay attention to when you need to rest in any area. Get to know your limits—physical, mental and emotional. Become more aware of the feedback your body and mind are constantly giving you.

For now, you will have only one three-month goal—the one you set for your number one priority.

Step Five

Now you are ready to write down goals for your second priority. The first goal that you will set is a six-month goal. The second is your nine-month goal. Stop there and go on to your third priority.

Step Six

The first goal you will set for the activity you listed third is a nine-month goal. This is the only goal you will write down at this time for this category.

COMPLETING THE TWO-YEAR HEALTH PLAN

Your first three categories are all you need to work with right now, and I recommend that you not go beyond the nine-month goal for each. Take your time in completing the rest of the two-year health plan. Take at least the next several weeks to outline the rest of your goals for the first three categories, as well as to set the goals for your fourth, fifth, and sixth-ranked priorities. Remember: The first goal for each is half of what you are now doing. If you are not doing anything in a particular area, then start with a minimal goal. Make the goals easier to meet than not to meet, and set goals that are concrete so that your progress is measurable. Remember, you want to set goals so that you would virtually have to try to fail in order not to meet them. You can always come back and revise them later.

I recommend that you review your plan at least every three months. Post it in a prominent place—on the refrigerator door, inside the bathroom cabinet. By the time the first nine months are up, you will find that you are thinking very differently about your life. Some of our patients are into their fifteenth year with their health plans, and still going strong.

Over the past twenty years I have had the opportunity to observe many patients reorganize their lives and experience long-term remissions from advanced cancers. Whatever the primary focus of their health plan at the beginning, over time the other areas invariably took on more importance and the primary area became somewhat less important. They develop a more balanced approach to life in general.

In the beginning, there tends to be more intensity, rigidity, and missionary zeal around our patients' activities. As they continue to experience good health, they shift to a more relaxed and confident approach. They tend to feel that what they have done is not so remarkable, and they frequently state that anyone can get well. All they need is a strong commitment to put these basic sound approaches to health to work.

Now let's look at some of the common questions and problems that arise when we start to work on plans.

Social Support

In this area, make sure your goals are not dependent on other people's initiatives. For example, if you want to spend more time talking with your adult children, don't make your goal "Ask the kids to call once a week," because they might not do it. Instead, make your goal something like "Attempt to make contact with each of my children once a week." This depends on your actions, not theirs.

Many patients set a goal of asking for help a certain number of times a week. This can be very difficult for them, because cancer-prone people often have a deep sense of not deserving help. It is important to change your habit of trying to do it all yourself. If you do set such a goal, remember that you accomplish it simply by asking. It doesn't matter whether the person you ask for help says yes or no.

If you intend to join a cancer support group, don't make just joining your goal; specify how many sessions per week or per month you will attend. Or agree to experiment with a support group for a certain number of meetings before you make a decision to join or leave. The more specific your goals are, the easier it is to measure your progress.

Some people think that reaching out for social support requires becoming more open and expressive than they are by nature. If you have always been reserved, move at your own pace. It is most important to increase your openness with *yourself* and to work with the feelings that arise. You can do this without giving up your privacy. A support group can also respect your need for privacy; there may well be other private people there who will welcome your presence.

Diet

Diet is an important part of getting well, because our natural ability to heal depends on proper nourishment. The nutrition guidelines we offer at the center are basic and well-known. Since the late 1970s, we have recommended the "Dietary Guidelines for Americans" published by the Surgeon General's office. These were adopted by the American Cancer Society and the National Cancer Institute several years later.

Summarized, the basics are as follows:

- an increase in fruits and vegetables, particularly fresh fruits and vegetables;
- a shift from red meat to more white meat;
- more fiber and roughage;
- less sugar, less salt, less fat and oil;
- caffeine at the equivalent of two cups of coffee per day or less;
- alcohol at the equivalent of two mixed drinks (two ounces of liquor) or less per day.

Notice that these are general directions only and allow a wide number of choices to be made.

At the Center, we concentrate primarily on our patients' attitude toward diet and nutrition. I believe this is more important than the exact details of what they eat. If you are making healthy changes in your diet, are you approaching them with enthusiasm and a sense of excitement? Or are you treating them as another dreary part of being ill, an obligation, or a sacrifice of something you used to enjoy? If you're on a stringent regimen and believe you must stick to it no matter what the consequences, you may not be helping yourself. It is healthier to agree to a diet with the attitude that you'll follow it for a period of time and then evaluate whether or not it is helping you feel better.

I have had patients who have insisted on staying on a particular diet that is obviously having detrimental effects upon their body until their health declines to a dangerous level, even until they die. I have seen other patients use the same diet and get well again.

Be especially careful that you are not using a diet to punish yourself for any past abuses with food. You want to focus on reward, not punishment. Give yourself a healthy diet as a reward for taking care of yourself and as a way of supporting yourself through this difficult time.

If you find yourself constantly hungry and tired, if you are continually frustrating yourself to stay on the diet you have chosen, or if you find yourself continually going off it, pay attention. Don't be afraid to consider changing the diet you initially chose. It may have served you well for a while, but it may be time to move on to another program that suits your present needs better.

Basically, you need to pay attention to your body— listen to what it is telling you. For example, Reid became a vegetarian for a while, but he soon found that he needed meat in his diet. This doesn't mean that everyone needs to eat meat; it means that Reid discovered that he felt better and had more energy after eating it. He also experimented with vitamins, starting out with a prescribed program, but gradually modifying it to suit his own response.

If you are in treatment, get as much information as you can about how it will affect your nutrition. The nurses who give the treatment regularly will have many tips about when to eat relative to treatment, which foods "set" the best, and so forth. Then, with experience, you can fine-tune your own reactions.

Remember that the body is both adaptable and continually changing. What tastes good to you one day may not the next. What you couldn't eat or didn't like years ago may taste good to you now. Eat what agrees with you! That sounds so simple, but many people ignore that simple way of selecting what they eat.

Exercise

Exercise is important, but one of our biggest problems is getting patients to slow down. Patients tend to overcommit to exercise programs that are too ambitious and inflexible.

Set your goals around exercise that you enjoy doing and that you will continue to do. Look at where you want to be in two years and begin to move in that direction in a very gentle way.

You want to stimulate your immune mechanisms through exercise, not exhaust yourself by doing too much too fast. Learn to move gently into exercise and listen to your body for feedback. The first ninety seconds of any exercise routine are the most important, because if you exhaust yourself right away, you won't be able to continue. So be particularly gentle and watch your breathing at the beginning of your session.

The most effective technique I have used with myself and my patients over the years is to strike up a conversation as I begin exercising. (Frequently this conversation is with myself, since I often exercise alone.) As soon as I have difficulty talking, I slow down or stop until I can again carry on a normal conversation. This signal is particularly important to watch during the first ninety seconds. It lets me know that I am doing too much too fast, and it is much easier than trying to monitor my pulse.

People may think you are a bit odd for talking to yourself—otherwise this is a very helpful tool.

I have helped many people with widely spread cancer develop exercise programs, showing them how to be particularly aware of breathing and discomfort so that they can use exercise as a healthy tool.

Even if you are confined to bed, it is helpful to imagine yourself engaged in physical activities you enjoy. In addition, move in bed within your limits of comfort. If you get up to go the the bathroom, count this as exercise. Hold on to your image of physical pleasure; it is another connection with life.

Right now, you can focus on stimulating your healing systems through exercise, not on extensive physical conditioning. Feeling good during physical activity and afterward is of primary importance. Remember that discomfort and pain are signals to slow down and stop!

Play

Many patients are surprised to find this a very difficult area for goal setting. Play is undervalued in our culture, and illness in the family tends to curtail it further. Some of our patients and their families have been scolded for having a good time: "You aren't taking your illness seriously enough," or "How can you enjoy yourself when your loved one is dying?" And yet play is one of the key components of creativity, and creativity is essential to the healing process.

As a fun exercise and a way to get started, begin to develop a list of forty playful activities, half of which cost less than five dollars each. It is important to have a long list of options, because, generally speaking, when you need to play the most, you have the hardest time thinking of something fun to do. Remember that what is playful for you one day is not necessarily playful on another day. One woman said that cooking is work if she is rushed to get dinner for the family after a day at the office, but cooking is play when she is on vacation and can explore interesting new recipes. Also, what is enjoyable for one person may not be enjoyable for another, so don't just list things that are generally considered play, list the things that give you the most pleasure. And finally, beware of playing as if it were work: We've all seen grim-faced people on the tennis court who would rather die than lose.

The amount of play that I suggest to our patients, the amount that I found right for myself many years ago and that I've stayed with, is one hour a day, seven days a week. This includes weekends, holidays, and vacations. (Before I recognized the importance of play, my vacations were filled with timetables and events requiring complex organization—just like work.) One hour a day can be an appropriate two-year goal. Now, how much are you playing currently?

At the Simonton Cancer Center, we've put together the following play list drawn up by our patients. After you've written down your own ideas, you may want to use the list to stimulate your imagination.

Play List

Visit friends
Play bridge
Go outdoors
Garden
Go to the country
Cook
Needlepoint
Sew
Watch football
Watch kids play sports
Take a day trip with the kids
Snowmobiling
Long talk with my husband/wife
Swimming
New York Times crossword puzzle
Parcheesi
Read gardening books
Write down family history
Clue, Monopoly, or Hangman
Sing Christmas carols
Make popcorn strings

Listen to music
Go horseback riding
Paint
Play cribbage
Do mental math
Play catch
Bridge
Motorcycling
Metal sculpture
Make pottery
Go sledding
Roughhousing
Finger painting
Play with building blocks
Sex, sexual fantasy
Erector sets
Plastic airplane models
Take photos
Build snowman
Make sand castle
Watch birds feed

Run our dog
Fly a kite
Sculpt
Tubing down a river
Walk along the creek
Go to a movie
Play backgammon
Gin Rummy
Listen to music
Dance
Go to a campus art show
Chant or listen to chanting
Cook a new dish
Play golf
Attend a school drama production
Explore a new store
Take a coffee break
Play miniature golf
Pop popcorn
Repair something
Tell someone a joke
Build a fire
Bike ride
Watch tadpoles evolve
Pull weeds after a rain
Cut the grass
Watch a TV comedy
Look at model homes
Go for a fabulous dinner
Send for refunds
Sit on the patio

Play hopscotch
Jump rope
Play jacks
Play squash
Go to the theater
Buy trinkets
Watch auto racing
Learn bonsai gardening
Play Frisbee
Play Simon Says
Play Bingo
Pinball machines
Jigsaw puzzles
Play pool
Feed the fish
Watch the sun set or rise
Woodworking
Go camping
Play chess or checkers
Go to the zoo
Go to the opera
Play in the surf
Go for a drive
Hike
Watch toads catch bugs
Go birdwatching
Play with clay
Watch the clouds
Draw
Have company over

Creative Thinking

As you already know, using meditation and imagery is a vital part of the work you'll be doing in this book. However, you don't want to make this a burdensome process. If you believe that meditation could become something you dread doing every day, start by trying it every other day, or even less. If you are just beginning to explore creative thinking, you also may not know where you want to be with meditation and imagery two years from now. Some of our patients set very broad goals in this area. For example, "(1) I want to understand more about meditation and imagery and be more comfortable with these techniques; and (2) I want to have incorporated meditation and imagery into my life."

As you become more aware of how your mind works and how you learn, you will find that many activities contribute to your creative thinking. Sometimes a patient really connects with this area first by reading a book on golf or tennis that discusses the mental aspects of the game. He or she begins to see the similarities to what we are asking them to do for their health. I play several instruments for fun, but learning a new piece also reminds me how much conscious effort and attention to individual notes are necessary before that wonderful moment when it all comes together in my unconscious and I begin to play smoothly. This is the same process we go through in learning new beliefs.

Purpose

Some patients identify their work or profession as their primary purpose in life, but many others do not. You may find that your hobby or your volunteer work or your friends or your family have more to do with your deepest purpose in being alive. In the letter series, you will see how this topic became increasingly important to Reid.

Your inner wisdom will be very valuable in clarifying your goals. Some people mistakenly think that they have to become different people, with new, more "noble" aims in life. In fact, what tends to unfold is related to what you are already doing—we are not where we are by accident. We are already on the path, we simply need to become more aware of it, to fine-tune and refocus our thinking. A man who identifies his purpose with his job may need to discover what parts of his job are most significant to him and seek ways to spend more time with those. A woman whose life has focused on being a good mother to her children may feel bereft because they are now on their own. But one of the most important parts of mothering is modeling—how she lives her own life. She can continue to be a mother at a deeper level.

Remember that your new sense of purpose does not invalidate your previous experience. Your purpose will probably continue to shift throughout life. Some of the shifts we see are very subtle. Or a person's external life may change relatively little, while the internal changes are huge.

We also do a great deal of work on purpose because illness often arises at critical times when our life purpose changes—when a previous focus, as a worker, parent, or spouse, for example, no longer fills our days. At these times, we need to translate our inner purpose into new circumstances. Purpose is part of our survival mechanism.

If you find yourself paralyzed at the thought of identifying some "significant" purpose, just ask yourself, "What is my strongest connection to life today?" What makes you feel most vital, most alive, most involved? Perhaps today is Halloween, and the answer comes, "Today, I am here to take my kids trick-or-treating." Enter into that purpose wholeheartedly.

A CRUCIAL BALANCE

In the last three chapters, you have gained some insight into three of the basic tools that we teach at the Simonton

Cancer Center: communicating with your support person and others; meditation and inner wisdom work; and developing a two-year health plan. Your skills in meditating and working with your inner wisdom will improve as you experiment with these processes. Your plan will help you stay focused, live more consciously, and make wiser decisions.

I believe that the speed of your healing, as well as the nature of your healing—whether it's short-term or long-term—depends on your imagination, attitude, beliefs, choices, decisions, and your will to live. As you begin to balance the physical, mental, and spiritual aspects of your life, I think you will be happier and find life more exciting and worthwhile. These changes will be reflected in your health. While neither Reid nor I can tell you how to get your life into balance, we can guide you toward that end.

TWO-YEAR PERSONAL HEALTH PLAN

3 months	6 months	9 months	12 months	15 months	18 months	21 months	24 months

STOP HERE FOR NOW
FINISH THE PLAN OVER
THE NEXT SEVERAL WEEKS

————— 6

Introduction to the Letter Series

How Reid Henson's Experience Can Help You

With Reid's letters, you are being offered the opportunity to take an intense look at another cancer patient's innermost thoughts and feelings, with the added benefit of having him point out to you what he believes was significant about his process of getting well. These letters are a wonderful body of work. I know of nothing else like them.

THE ORIGIN

Following his miraculous recovery in 1981, people began to hear about what happened to Reid, and they were curious about this miracle. Cancer patients would call or visit, and Reid would talk with them for hours. They always asked the same questions: What should I do to get well?

Reid didn't know the answer to that question, he only knew what he had done. He didn't feel comfortable telling people what to do with their lives, especially when he knew they were in life-threatening situations.

However, Reid kept having the urge to write something down, but he didn't know what. He would be awakened early in the morning, around five o'clock, and feel that he should go downstairs and write; but for a long time he didn't. Then one morning, in response to such an urge, he got up, went downstairs to his office, and picked up his pen. He wrote for hours, putting down thoughts much as he had when he received the message about parenting after his son was arrested. This was the birth of the letter series.

Shortly after Reid finished about fifteen letters, he began to run out of ideas. He thought he didn't have anything more to say. Later on, he realized that he had misunderstood some things about his cancer experience, and as a result, the energy and wisdom for the letter series had simply been halted.

As he once again began to grow in understanding, as he continued to study and observe himself and the world around him, the mysterious stimulus for writing the letters returned, as did the ideas.

Reid brought these letters to me and asked me to help him with them. We reviewed them carefully and worked on them for months before he started sending them out to cancer patients. Soon, by word of mouth only, people from around the world began to request that their names be added to Reid's mailing list, and we began offering the letters to some of the cancer patients who called the Simonton Cancer Center. Within a year, Reid began getting wonderful feedback, patients writing to say that they were experiencing miraculous changes in their health and in their lives.

I believe that anyone can learn from Reid's willingness to explore and experience the miraculous. The responses to his letters have been a good indication of that. Reid is telling you what he did, he's not telling you what to do. Remember always that what helps one person can harm another. You need to follow your own path, not someone else's. Let the experiences of Reid and others help you on your way, but don't try to walk their path.

One of the most wonderful things about Reid's letters is that although he is sharing his experiences around cancer, his message seems to have strong appeal to people who are suffering from all kinds of problems. He has heard from people addicted to drugs, people going through divorce, people who have had a recent death in the family, and people with almost every type of illness from allergies to AIDS, who find that his letters have stimulated healthful changes in their lives. Since my expertise is in working with cancer patients, I will be directing my comments to cancer patients; however, no matter who you are or what your problem, I think these letters can be a help and comfort to you.

THE PURPOSE OF THE LETTERS

It has been my experience that while many patients are willing to make changes to save their lives, these changes are often temporary or isolated. Healing from cancer requires profound, lasting changes. In the deepest sense, healing from cancer is healing your life, and that is an ongoing project, not something you can do overnight.

I have found that patients who examine their core beliefs and consider, or reconsider, such issues as their purpose in life and their beliefs about God, often experience deep changes that create a new physical, mental, and spiritual balance that is conducive to health. Creating this environment seems to require frequently repeated, positive and productive stimuli over a long period of time. In other words, you need continuous encouragement that urges you to act on your health in a positive way. That's what we hope this letter series is going to provide for you.

LONG-TERM SURVIVORS

I sometimes say that the only thing common to all long-term survivors is that they are all long-term survivors. Since each of us is unique, each of our processes is unique, and that is true for each long-term survivor.

Our society has a great aptitude for gathering information and compiling statistics on the number of people with cancer, the number who survive, the number who die, the percentage living in a certain area who get cancer, and so on. One of the problems with this approach is that the information doesn't apply to you as an individual. You can't know which side of the statistics you are on, so they are meaningless to you. Perhaps only one person in a thousand survives some rare disease, but if it's you, that disease is 100 percent survivable for you.

I suggest you forget the statistics you've heard for whatever type of cancer you are experiencing. You are not like all the other people who are experiencing or have experienced that cancer—you are you, a unique individual. You are doing important things to enhance whatever treatment you have chosen. You are using mental and spiritual processes to make that treatment work for you. And while we now have statistics about the positive impact of therapy and other mental processes, we don't have statistics on spiritual approaches. We don't yet know what bringing spiritual elements into the healing of cancer translates to in numbers. However, I think you are much more likely to experience a miracle or spontaneous recovery if you believe it is possible! I have experienced this with one patient after another through the years. While you may not believe in miracles and can't conceive of actually experiencing a miracle, we are going to work on that possibility just as we worked on your beliefs about cancer.

Reid's letters offer you an opportunity to reevaluate cancer and the healing of cancer in a way that can be meaningful and useful to you. I want to emphasize the word "useful." This is not a philosophy book, this is a how-to book. Use it, don't just read it. If you just read the book, it's not going to be nearly as effective as it can be if you do the work.

DOING THE WORK

When I first met Reid, one of the things that concerned me immediately was the amount of fear he was experiencing. I still remember the intense look of fear in his eyes that day. Yes, that fear motivated him to act, but resolving that fear was central to his getting well. Intense fear is stressful, a killer. Moving past it is crucial to moving toward health. Reid was willing to change the beliefs that were producing that fear. He was also very committed to doing whatever else was required to get well.

Right now, you may be overwhelmed and immobilized by your fear of cancer or of dying. To move through that, you need to begin to do the work in this book, proceeding at a pace that is comfortable for you. Meditation on a regular basis can provide a quiet time to take a break from worrying, a time when you can focus on healthy thoughts. If you have yet to try the meditation exercises in Chapter 4, I urge you to do so before you begin the letter series. Meditation and imagery can be very useful in contemplating the subjects presented in Reid's letters. Your inner wisdom can also be very helpful, so if you've yet to become aware of your inner wisdom, continue to work on that.

Hopefully, by now you have also begun to develop a play list. It is crucial to take the time to play, even if you haven't set up a goal for that in your two-year health plan. Do something fun before, during, or after the time that you do work around your health.

SUGGESTIONS FOR WORKING WITH THE LETTERS

Reid and I ask you to use the letters as they are designed to be used. If you just read them straight through, you're not going to get nearly as much from them as you will if you use them more creatively.

When Reid began mailing the letters from his home, he sent them out to everyone on his list once a week. That gave each person seven days to read and reread each letter, an entire week to think about the material and to experiment with the ideas and suggestions.

Although you have access to all of the letters, we still suggest that you read the same letter each day for seven days, or at least for several days, before proceeding to the next. Each letter contains key points related to core beliefs that can play a pivotal role in helping to shift your perspective. If you read the letters straight through, you may feel overwhelmed by all this new material. But if you will work with just one letter for a period of time, you will probably find that you are able to address key issues and begin to shift your beliefs in a direction that is good for your health.

You need a reasonable amount of time to integrate each new concept into your thinking. As your perspective starts to shift, that shift will provide fertile ground for the next concept to take hold.

If you decide to read ahead, as I'm sure many of you will want to do, remember why we are asking you to stay with each letter and work with them in order—they are designed to build a new foundation for you, strengthening the base from which you live your life, one step at a time.

Just reading the letters a week at a time will be helpful. However, they will be even more effective if you actively participate in integrating them into your thinking. Take notes. Write in the margin of the book. Keep a journal. Make tapes. Let this be a continually active process. Your willingness to do the work, your determination to get better, the amount of time you spend, and the level on which you participate will all be important.

I think you will find that some letters have more value for you than others. You may want to spend more than a week when a topic addresses your particular interests or needs.

If you are too ill to read the letters, ask someone to read them aloud or tape them for you. If you are too ill to make notes, put your thoughts on tape. If you're too ill to tape your thoughts, just meditate on them and use your inner wisdom to help you explore them further. It may be helpful simply to repeat the basic meditation processes you learned in Chapter 4 one or more times during each week, making notes on the images you get each time. Notice whether or not the images change as you receive new information. Remember that you can also intentionally change your images to whatever you want them to be. Write down the images, and identify those that give you a particularly strong sense of power in your healing work.

You may find in some cases that you totally disagree with what Reid thinks and does. You don't have to agree with him to get well again. In fact, disagreeing is a form of participation. But don't just dismiss what Reid says, make some notes on why you disagree.

Or maybe you don't know if you agree or disagree with Reid's approach. That's okay, too. Experiment with some of the things he tried and see if they work for you.

After one or more letters covering a particular subject, I'll comment on Reid's approach and offer you some alternatives. With my comments and suggestions, you'll be able to give yourself a checkup on how you're doing with this work. Unlike the letters, you need not read these comments for seven days. You may read them after completing your work on the previous letter, or you can jump ahead to my comments if you find a section particularly difficult.

You will find that the subjects and statements are repeated in the letters and in my comments. The repetition is intentional. I know that when you are not feeling well, it is often hard to concentrate. That's why we ask you to read each letter several times, and that's one reason why we repeat or highlight important statements. We want to make sure that you have more than one opportunity to consider and integrate key concepts.

I think it is wonderful that Reid is willing to have these letters published, to be so public about his life and his beliefs. He is open and honest about who he was and is, and he is willing to be vulnerable to the judgment of others in order to share his experiences and be of help. I hope you will receive each of his letters into your heart as though Reid is a special messenger with a special message addressed to you personally.

Reid and I want you to know that we support you, we want you to get well. But more importantly, we believe that the whole universe is supporting you in your efforts. You are here on this earth for a reason. You are here to make your own special contribution, whatever that contribution may be. It is in the best interests of the universe that you experience your own unique joy and deep satisfaction. We hope we can help you do that, and we hope that we have enabled you to begin this exciting adventure with a deep sense of wonder and curiosity.

PART *II*

THE LETTERS OF REID HENSON

_____ ONE

Becoming a Student of Life

Dear Friend,

I am happy to share with you some ideas that have helped me realize some significant changes in my attitudes or points of view about life. At first I found it difficult to see things from any perspective other than those I had been stuck in for years.

I was slow to realize and accept the need for change. I believe this reflected my reluctance to see the truth about my innermost self. Although I found I had many undesirable qualities, in retrospect I see that I also had and have a lot of good ones, too. But for some reason, early in my cancer experience, the negatives tended to dominate my consciousness and made taking a close look at myself seem most unpalatable.

As I think about it now, it seems clear to me that my fear of change reflected in large measure my fear of my innermost self. I suspected there was something deep within that deserved to die, and I was not prepared to face it. I saw death approaching and felt that there must be something I could change about myself or my life that would keep this from happening. I had to change to avoid death, and yet I was afraid to change because I didn't know what changes would lead to in my life. Both alternatives were frightening to me, but death more so than the other. I can now see that the fear of death was one of the most powerful stimulators leading to change in my life.

An idea that I found enormously helpful in making healthy changes was to assume the perspective of a "student of life." As a student of life, I became an independent observer of myself, or "Reid." With my new point of view, I began to practice seeing each event in "Reid's" life as a learning opportunity. Instead of judging each event as either good or bad, I tried to remain objective and see that some experiences are simply more difficult than others. I also tried to remember that I did not have all the facts. When I forgot to play this student role as "Reid's" life unfolded, I found it helpful later to look back at what had happened to "Reid," becoming aware of what might be learned in retrospect. I began to see that things did not always turn out as I expected.

I found that my new point of view relieved me of any need to change the world—to change events, people, or whatever. I began to see myself as learning from all aspects of life. I also began to view others as fellow students of life along with me, irrespective of how they saw themselves. This made it easier for me to begin to accept others as they are.

I did not experience these changes overnight, but changes did come and there is little doubt that the changes I experienced were good for me. Using the student approach, I was gradually able to move at a more comfortable and enjoyable pace through life. Being a student seemed to entail little stress because it allowed me to experience life freely, without feeling that I had to control that which I could not control anyway. I needed change within myself, but I had been wasting my time and energy trying to change others, as well as life's past and future events.

Before I became a student of life, I was concerned about

every decision I made, and there was little relief from this self-generated anxiety. I finally realized that regardless of the outcome of my decisions, as a student I could benefit from any decisions I made if I learned from the experience.

I found I made more progress with less stress if I concerned myself only with whatever decision was at hand, focusing on the present and making a clear choice. I realized that while each choice would have consequences, I could always evaluate those consequences, learn from them and choose again.

This reduced the level of stress in my life because it enabled me to focus on the choices relevant now, while realizing things wouldn't necessarily turn out as expected. I became more aware that future choices were yet to be presented, and past choices had already been made. Consequently, the only choices I could really deal with were those before me in the here and now.

I started trying to be more conscious from moment to moment, asking myself "What is going on right now?" and "What can I do about it?" Often the only choice available was to sit back, observe "Reid," and learn.

As I became more attuned to experiencing life rather than trying to control it, I became more and more comfortable with the "unexpected." This helped me to move from my current understanding into unknown territory to gather, consider, and store new information that could change the way I was experiencing life.

As I moved more and more deeply into my student role, I became increasingly comfortable with the idea of considering death simply as another change. I came to believe that death is just another transitional experience through which I will graduate into a different school which will continue to present the lessons I need. I began to realize that God had provided very well for me in this experience.

This gave me confidence that God would continue to do so in whatever came next. My fear of change and my fear of death eventually subsided.

Since I had cancer, I explored many ideas, points of view, and experiences. I acted. I chose, evaluated, learned, and then chose again.

Comments on Letter One

Underlying the student-of-life concept are several of Reid's core beliefs: He believes that there is something to be learned from life; he believes that there is a creative force (or forces) in the universe attempting to teach us something from our life experiences; and he believes that this life force is caring and loving and has created this learning process to benefit us and our universe. These beliefs were obviously healthy beliefs for Reid in his cancer experience.

The student concept has been a part of many spiritual traditions, but it was new to Reid. It became an important tool because it enabled him to look at his illness and his life from an objective point of view. When one is objective, one is in a neutral state emotionally, which, as we have discussed, stimulates the body's healing systems.

In evaluating the student-of-life concept for your own use, consider that it allowed Reid to begin to experience his life more fully since he was, in a sense, giving himself permission to experience whatever emotions and thoughts came up for him. He no longer felt he had to control or avoid them in order to prevent being overwhelmed. Instead, he could feel and think them, yet still maintain some safe distance through objective observation.

This can be an important area of work for you because, as a cancer patient, you may be struggling to get more control over your life at a time when you feel betrayed by your body. If your life seems out of control right now or you feel you are losing control, make a concerted effort to develop more trust in yourself and in your ability to heal.

Take small steps to influence your life and health, rather than trying to gain complete control.

I empathize with those of you who would like to get control quickly, thinking that by doing so, you'll get immediate physical results. I recognize this problem easily in my patients because I have it myself. I tend to do things too fast and to excess: play to excess, exercise to excess, and work to excess. It has taken me a long time to balance my life, and it still goes out of balance from time to time. I am fortunate in having people around me to remind me when I stray and who support my efforts when I attempt to regain my balance. My greatest help, however, is my own awareness.

The student of life approach is an excellent method for building awareness. Here are a couple of simple ways to begin to practice the student approach:

• *Keep a journal.* At the end of each day, look back at the thoughts and emotions that came up during the day's activities. Write down what you learn from looking at your thoughts and emotions in retrospect. Be especially aware of how your thoughts and beliefs create emotions.

Or, as a student of life, look back at your experiences with cancer. Write down what you think and how you feel about what you've learned thus far. Keep these notes to evaluate your progress as you learn more. Remember: Your emotions are a result of your beliefs and thoughts, so if you want to feel better, you need to think healthier.

• If you haven't done so before, *make a list of things that make you feel better.* Ask yourself directly, "What can I do to improve the way I feel?" Do one of those things today, approaching it as a student of life. Do this as an exercise in learning to trust that you can influence the way you feel by taking action and practicing healthy beliefs.

Reid couldn't control his life after becoming a student of life any more than he had before, but he let go of the need to control it by experiencing life from an objective, neutral viewpoint. A healthy unconscious attitude toward life's events emerged from his new belief that life is the teacher and he is a student.

Whenever you choose to use it, the student perspective can give you the freedom to acknowledge all your thoughts and feelings, especially the difficult, negative ones. When you feel free to experience negative thoughts and emotions, it is likely that you will gain some understanding into how you created them—an insight you would miss if you resisted or repressed those thoughts.

The ultimate goal is to select which thoughts you want to hold and which ones you want to change. You can achieve this by continuing to examine your beliefs and by changing your beliefs to produce positive or neutral emotions. This is a life-long process, an ideal to move toward rather than something to accomplish all at once. One step that you can take in that direction is simply to practice holding uplifting thoughts. Any time spent in doing this helps shift you into a relaxed or neutral state and makes a positive contribution to your health.

Here is a practical exercise in this area:

• This week *experiment with being aware of negative emotions*—specifically anger, fear, or hopelessness. When you become aware that you are experiencing one of these emotions, stop and immediately write down the belief that is producing that emotion. Remember, the aim is not to suppress the emotion, but to work with it. Use the exercise for emotional mastery in Chapter 4 as often as you need it.

It took Reid a long time, and he went through many experiences and got a lot of professional help, before he was able to change his unhealthy beliefs, thoughts, and resulting emotions. Take your time, do the work at your own pace, pay attention to how you feel, and only do what you have the desire and energy to do right now.

_____ *TWO*

Blaming, Authority, and Control

Dear Friend,

I didn't make much progress until I focused my resources on the real problems within myself. Blaming others had kept me from doing that for years. I had a strong habit of blaming other people for the problems I experienced in life. I know this is a rather common human tendency, but I found it to be a very unhealthy one for me. It made me feel I was a helpless victim of all sorts of things beyond my control.

This was dangerous because while I was blaming others for my predicament, I was making little or no progress in solving the problems at hand. These unsolved problems kept accumulating, and the burden became progressively greater as time passed. I could see that blaming had not improved my life and was not likely to do so in the future.

As I look back on my life before experiencing cancer, I am amazed to realize how difficult it was for me to deal with a wide variety of situations. I had the view that if I didn't solve the problems I encountered, I was a failure. I found this to be a very stressful point of view because I found it impossible to "fix" all those other people who were "causing" me to have all those problems.

As a result of thinking I knew what was best, it often seemed reasonable to me that someone or something caused some ill event to occur. Whoever or whatever that was should be blamed because they or it were wrong. They or it needed to be penalized and corrected. I was often aggravated by having to waste time correcting something that I felt should have been right to begin with.

In many instances, I had decided that I knew what was good, best, or even ideal for everyone involved. Of course, I really didn't know all of the intentions, priorities, or interrelationships of the people or events involved in the circumstances I encountered. But I often found it quite easy to overlook this lack of information and understanding.

However, as I began to apply my student point of view to blaming, things began to look rather different. As a student, I was focusing my attention on learning rather than blaming. This meant I focused more on what was actually happening than on what I imagined should be happening. Since I saw myself as learning from whatever happened, it seemed contradictory to be thinking negatively (blaming) about the people and events I was learning from.

I still saw things I didn't feel were right, but from a somewhat more positive point of view. I found that the concept of responsibility could be used in place of *blame*. It may appear to you that I am splitting hairs with these words, but please bear with me on these important points:

• If I saw someone as *blameworthy* in a particular situation, I also felt negatively toward them and tended to feel they should be punished for their dastardly deeds.

• If, on the other hand, I chose to see the same person as *responsible*, it cast them in a somewhat more positive light; a person could be either good or bad while being responsible.

As I practiced using "is responsible" in place of "is to blame," I began to realize that responsibility and authority seemed to go together. If I blamed someone for my situation or unhappiness, then I was also letting that person have authority over me. If I gave the authority over certain aspects of my life to others, I unintentionally surrendered my own power to choose freely and to be responsible for myself.

In effect, I realized I was giving others the control I had once sought for myself. Having already put the inclination to control aside in some measure, I could see that assuming full responsibility for my own experiences actually facilitated my learning process. As a student of life, this made sense to me.

While I was stuck in the habit of blaming, things often seemed hopeless, and I felt helpless to do anything productive under the circumstances as I perceived them. For me, blaming seemed to activate a subconscious process that conjured up negative feelings, feelings that indicated someone should be punished.

The really shocking part of what I learned was that when I blamed myself for something, these same subconscious forces were unleashed against me. Blame, I found, is a double-edged sword. If I blame someone for my situation, then my anger is directed toward that person, who I feel must be punished. If I blame myself, I am both the origin and the recipient of the blame and punishment. So I learned that blaming either others or myself was unproductive and produced feelings of unworthiness and depression.

Even after I realized that blaming myself and/or others was unproductive, it was hard to adopt a new point of view. Somewhere during this period, I began to use the student concept more effectively. I decided to experiment with the idea that none of the people I was blaming indeed deserved blame. They were, in fact, doing the best they could with the information and understanding they had at the time. It was in experimenting with this idea that I realized we are all in the same boat. I saw all of mankind as being here on earth to learn and grow toward an understanding of life. Thus, blame gradually became a less useful concept, since all here on earth are learning just like me. This also meant that there was no need to blame myself. I was a student and students learn, at least in part, through trial and error. Error, making a mistake, became the prelude to learning rather than a trigger to set off blaming.

As I think back on it now, it seems to me that many aspects of my tendency to blame myself rested on the idea of control. Since I felt I was or should have been in control of everything, it seemed logical to blame myself for things I saw as less than ideal. I should be able to make things perfect, and when I couldn't, I blamed myself. No wonder life became so burdensome for me! I would have had to live in Utopia to avoid things for which I could blame myself.

I gradually realized I was not in control of my life because I was continuously interacting with other people and events over which I had no control. It was obviously contradictory to think I could control my own life if I could not control all the things that influenced my life in one way or another. I could, however, exercise control over how I responded to each circumstance as it developed.

In time, the tendency to blame myself (and others) began to diminish in strength. I began to concentrate on responding to life as a student, observing life as it unfolded. The same old things were happening, but I began to see more of them as learning opportunities rather than as opportunities to blame myself or others. As I took advantage of more and more of these learning opportunities, I found myself changing and growing more rapidly. Life became more interesting and more exciting. I began to feel better, too.

_____ *THREE*

Guilt, Error, and Growth

Dear Friend,

One day a remarkable insight came to me during a prayer and meditation period that was especially meaningful. Upon emerging from this deeply relaxed state, I got up to make a couple of notes and was quite surprised to find myself drawing complex diagrams and writing page after page about the subject of guilt.

I made a series of notes, each one leading to the next: "If I am guilty, I should be punished. The severity of the punishment should be commensurate with the crime. My behavior has resulted in the ruin of other lives, therefore my life should be ruined. I should have a problem even worse than the problems of those whose lives I have ruined. I have leukemia. No medical treatment can be effective. My life should be ended. I am dying. The scales of divine justice will be balanced as a result."

This overall picture of my thought processes in relation to my illness seemed to be based on the concept of "an eye for an eye." Thus the punishment had to ruin my life, and leukemia seemed appropriate.

It was shocking to uncover such thinking within myself. In fact, I had been afraid to delve into my subconsciousness because I suspected something unpalatable would be uncovered, and I was right.

On the other hand, I was encouraged because I now had something very specific to work on. It appeared to me that guilt was one of the main roots of some of my most severe problems. So I addressed each of the issues about which I knew I felt guilty.

I found that I felt guilty about all sorts of things, including my divorce, the death of my infant son, and my older son's addiction to drugs. I began to reexamine my responsibilities in each situation.

Insofar as the divorce was concerned, I realized I had chosen the women I had dated, chosen to marry one of them, and had then chosen to divorce. I was responsible for my actions and inactions in this marriage. I had done the best I could, considering my level of understanding at the time, as I am sure was true of my ex-wife. No one benefitted from our feelings of guilt over our divorce.

My second child by that marriage died at birth. Since my wife was in the hospital, I went alone to a funeral home to select a casket for our baby. I then rode hundreds of miles on a train with my dead son, to take him to my hometown. A funeral and graveside service followed. I'm sure you can appreciate the deep agony I felt. I just could not understand how an innocent child could die at birth. Why did it happen? Was it something I had done? Why did I feel so guilty?

There had been indications that the baby had some abnormalities. I began to think about that. Maybe a wisdom far beyond mine knew that his body was just not suitable for life on this planet. I finally accepted his death as an event in my life to be experienced and studied. I found that after looking back at this tragedy, I could move on with a greater respect for the life force that created the universe and all that is in it. Somehow it just didn't make sense to me that a force that could create the universe could be wrong about anything. I would just have to trust that, although the reason my infant son died was beyond my understanding, he was somehow taken care of by a higher power.

I also began to look more closely at what was going on with my first son and his drug addiction. I believed that I had messed up his life and that his addiction was my fault. I believed that I had been a poor husband, which led to the divorce, which caused his addiction. Again, I began to try to see myself as I now looked at others: I had done the best I could do with the understanding I had at the time. I had made mistakes, lots of mistakes, but I could also see that I had not used drugs myself, and I certainly hadn't bought any for my son. He had found it difficult to deal with the realities he faced, and he had chosen to use drugs as an escape mechanism. That was his choice. Although it wasn't how I wanted him to lead his life, I knew that I was not in control of his life (or even my own, for that matter).

In reexamining these issues, I began to see guilt as the fruit of my conscience, guiding me to reexamine my past choices and to make healthier ones in the future. I found that guilt could be an important alarm, telling me that a choice I was making was not in harmony with my conscience.

I also found that I had not given due significance to the many factors that had had a bearing on each situation. Consequently, I had been judging myself guilty for causing many difficulties over which I actually had little influence. I bore some responsibility, but so did many other people, circumstances, and events. Clearly, I was not in full control.

I believe you will now understand why I see guilt as one of the key stimulants leading to my illness. It was interesting to observe the timing of improvements in my health in relation to my progress in coming to grips with my guilt.

Many people I have talked with think I shouldn't emphasize one's personal role and at least partial responsibility for illness, because it leads to a heavy guilt burden. I do not agree! As a student of life, I chose responsibility for my life and my illness, and with that came the responsibility and authority to do something about both. In effect, I gave myself permission to use my God given ability to choose again. This decision did not increase my guilt; instead it increased my understanding of life and relieved me from the guilt I had been feeling for many years. I chose anew to see my errors as poor choices made by a student of life who was continuing to learn and grow. I found that seeing errors as a natural part of the learning process was much better for me than feeling guilty and deserving of punishment. I also found responsibility much more productive than the hopeless outlook that comes from feeling like a victim.

Comments on Letters Two and Three

Blaming seems to be an American hobby, a thought process that is all too common in our Western culture. We all seem to spend much of our time figuring out who is right and who is wrong.

Reid used his student-of-life approach as a way of moving out of blaming and into a state of mind that was more productive for him. As a student of life, he considered blame to be a lesson that life was bringing him. This is a powerful approach for several reasons.

From his student perspective, he was able to look at blame objectively—he wasn't judging himself for blaming, but observing the nature of blame.

As Reid pointed out, you need to be careful not to turn from blaming other people for your illness to blaming yourself. Feeling guilty is a warning sign that you are blaming yourself. If you believe that cancer is some sort of punishment, it is very important that you replace this belief with one that is healthier. Continue to work with the first meditation in Chapter 4 on changing your beliefs about cancer. Make a conscious effort to see cancer not as punishment but as negative feedback, a message you can use to improve your life. The concept of negative feedback is healthy because it diminishes the feeling that cancer is controlling your life and puts it into perspective. Your life experience is not cancer; it does include cancer. To continue to believe that cancer is a form of punishment would not be conducive to your health.

As Reid pointed out, neither blaming nor guilt is pro-

ductive, but taking responsibility is. Responsibility em-
powers you to do something about your recovery, whereas
blame and guilt keep you locked in a rigid structure of anger
and hopelessness. Approaching blame and guilt from the
student perspective will help you see these areas objectively.
We primarily create guilt and blame from the unhealthy use
of "shoulds." We say, "I should have done that." "He
shouldn't have done what he did."

As an exercise in recognizing your thoughts and emotions about your illness, write down who or what you blame
for making you ill, and how you feel about that person or
thing or circumstance. You may blame people who have
made your life stressful. You may blame your parents or
family for a genetic predisposition to cancer. You may
blame your environment. You may blame yourself. You may
not even know you have thoughts of blame or guilt until you
look for them. Do this as a creative exercise to discover your
buried feelings and thoughts. Don't do anything with the
list other than observe the thoughts and emotions that
come with creating it.

After you've completed your list, you may discover that
even if you believe someone or something in particular is
the direct cause of your cancer, that information is of no
help to you. At this point, whoever or whatever it was is in
the past, and all you can deal with is what is going on right
now. Therefore, you may find it helpful to adopt the point
of view that there is no one and nothing to blame for your
illness, including yourself. Try to look at your illness only as
what you are experiencing right now, without connecting it
to anyone or anything. Try to see the cancer as "what is,"
rather than in the context of cause and effect. When you
can start from "Cancer is what I am experiencing right
now," then you can begin to move more productively toward becoming healthy without being hung up in blame

and guilt. In other words, for right now, *don't look so much at what made you sick as at what can make you well.*

Studying blame doesn't have to be a totally serious project. You can have some fun with it. Make a list of everything that's ever gone wrong in your life from the time you were born. Next to each item, write the person you can or would like to blame for that wrong. Then write down what this person would have to do for you to even the score. This gives you permission to feel blame while allowing you to observe the nature of blame at the same time.

You may find, as Reid did, that blame arises out of an issue of control—e.g. "Who is in control of what has happened to me and my health and my life?"

Feeling in control is feeling that what is happening in your life is consistent with the way you think life should be. When your experiences are not compatible with your beliefs, you may feel out of control, and you may want to blame someone or something for that feeling. Pay close attention to your beliefs and feelings about control, and note how they are associated with blame.

Gradually, you may find that in taking responsibility through your thoughts and actions, you are in the process of claiming your powers to influence your health. You may then feel more in control—or more comfortable being out of control. You will have a better sense of what you can change, and what you can't. Either way, you are likely to unhook yourself from the process of blaming. And remember, one of the best ways to eliminate guilt and blame is to remind yourself that all of us are always doing the best we can with the information and understanding that we have at that time. This is very important.

_____ FOUR

Malignant Beliefs and Malignant Realities

Dear Friend,

I had purchased and used a large number of self-help programs to achieve success in my business life. They came to have a new purpose when I put what I had learned from them into the context of my cancer experience. Although I have not carefully restudied these programs, I don't recall a single one that didn't focus considerable attention on the power of belief. A central theme in many of these courses is that our beliefs are powerful determinants in achieving or failing to achieve what we define as success in our lives.

I want to review with you some of the beliefs I had at the beginning of my cancer experience. I believed I was guilty of violating many of what I understood to be God's laws. Since I was guilty, I felt the need for commensurate punishment. I believed I had ruined another person's life, my son's, so I deserved to have my own life ended. Thus a "terminal" disease was appropriate for me, and no medical procedures could be allowed to work, because if they did heal me, "divine justice" would be thwarted.

Since I believed that I was somewhat at odds with God, I saw myself as being on my own in a hostile world where I would be punished somehow for the long list of misdeeds for which I felt guilty.

To say the least, I had some rather poorly thought out and very frightening views about the world and the nature of the creative force. I devoted a lot of time to reconsidering some of my old beliefs and how the mind uses beliefs.

I found it to be especially productive to write down what I had previously accepted as true about various things. (I defined "belief" as my perception or interpretation of some aspect of life.) I store such beliefs or truths at a subconscious level, and they operate automatically thereafter. The fact that they are subconscious implies that I am not routinely aware of their existence or operation. However, beliefs produce thoughts, and those thoughts flow into the conscious aspect of my mind. I am, at that point, aware of them.

This definition of belief helped me to understand that subconscious structures played a big role in my illness. I came to realize that the reason I could think new and healthy thoughts but would eventually drift back to something negative was that I had not altered my subconscious beliefs, which continued to operate just as they always had. I saw that many of the beliefs I had accepted were unreliable and unhealthy in my cancer experience. In fact, I would say some of my beliefs were so negative as to be termed malignant; I believe they eventually produced malignant realities in my life. As I see it, those involving guilt and the related need for punishment were especially damaging. Consequently, it seemed clear that I needed to reexamine and change my subconscious beliefs if I could.

Since I believed that my beliefs could play such a significant role in my healing, I devoted a lot of time to studying my mind and how beliefs might be created and stored. Here are some of my conclusions:

• My mind is a vastly complex mechanism, and I realize that complete understanding of it is beyond my capabilities.

• My beliefs are stored in my subconscious mind, and these beliefs become grouped together into belief structures that interact automatically to generate thoughts.

• My thoughts can be energized or de-energized if I am consciously aware of what I am thinking. This awareness leads me to a distinction. When I am aware—in other words, when I am acting as a student of life—I can observe "Reid's" thought processes. I can agree or disagree with the thoughts produced by "Reid's" mind. I can choose which thoughts I want to energize by agreeing with those thoughts, and I can choose which thoughts I want to de-energize by disagreeing with those thoughts. In so doing, I am able to choose which of "Reid's" beliefs or thoughts will be allowed to manifest in "Reid's" life experience. (At first, however, it was impossible for me to be alert enough to do this for more than a few minutes at a time.)

• My spiritual aspect translates my choices into physical reality in a way that is also beyond my understanding.

Despite the progress in my understanding, it was taking an enormous amount of time to pursue the many facets of my mind through self-hypnosis and meditation. It seemed that it would take a lifetime to painstakingly explore the whole labyrinth of subconscious processes and beliefs. I didn't think I would live long enough to complete my studies.

If that wasn't enough, another gigantic issue surfaced about the same time. I asked myself, "How can a mind that contains erroneous and unhealthy beliefs from the past be relied on to change and select valid and healthy beliefs now?" It seemed impossible to me. The only mind I had to work with was erroneous in some serious ways. I really didn't have much confidence in my mind once I knew some of the beliefs it contained.

Physically, I was going downhill rapidly. Now I had

come up against a brick wall in trying to find a mental solution to my health problems. I decided that the answers would have to come from the spiritual dimension, since it was the only one I had not explored in any significant way.

_____ *FIVE*

Choosing a Response to Cancer More Powerful Than Cancer Itself

Dear Friend,

Most people find it shocking when I say that I now see cancer as a blessing because it was the key stimulus that moved me closer to God. I see cancer, as well as all other adversity in my life, as a precious gift from God helping me to better understand my role in life in relation to him.

In essence, I believe that I chose a response to cancer—God—that was more powerful than the cancer itself. I figured curing my cancer would be easy for God. Since God created everything there is, he could surely create new cells in my body.

I saw this response—choosing God—to the adversity in my life as being much more important than the specific problem (cancer) to which I was responding. In a way, I was forced into this thinking and into a lot of other new concepts. As it became apparent that other human beings could not solve my health problem for me, I sought God and he responded. In my view, this change is the cornerstone of my recovery.

Once I invited the spiritual aspect of me into the problem, I found that Spirit can transform the human mind. It was only then that I realized I did not have to figure out all aspects of my illness in order to get well. At this point, my approach shifted from mental analysis toward developing trust in the spiritual dimension.

In doing so, I chose a response to cancer that enabled me to see this illness as an opportunity for a "student of life" to learn some much needed lessons.

One of the key lessons was to see the very definite limitations of my human mental processes. My mind can link together various beliefs into new associations and thereby seem to be creative, but I gradually realized that these new creations were really new assemblies of what was already present in my mind. I also found that spiritual input from the creative force could easily be limited or distorted by my existing beliefs. It seemed, in fact, that my mind tended to block those things it was not yet ready to deal with.

As these mental limitations became more apparent, I began to realize more deeply that some form of spiritual contact was essential. I was using meditation, progressive relaxation, and prayer in trying to find a solution to my health problems. But even at this stage, I was relying heavily on my mental powers while searching for a seemingly elusive spiritual reality.

I had always believed in God, but for most of my life, I couldn't make sense of spiritual things, so I had chosen just to ignore the whole subject. I knew I would have to deal with my personal spirituality some day, but I wasn't in any hurry to get around to it. Cancer changed that. All the physical evidence suggested I was going to meet my creator pretty soon, ready or not. The time to get ready was clearly at hand.

_____ *SIX*

Religion as a Gateway

Dear Friend,

I attended Sunday School and church quite regularly when I was growing up, but without much enthusiasm. I learned about the things I "should" do, but I wasn't able to make them a consistent part of my behavior. I felt both unsuccessful and guilty as a result.

I remember praying for various things that just did not come to pass. I felt unable to make religion work for me, and it was keeping me from trying lots of things that seemed appealing. I couldn't see that it had any benefits. I finally decided religion was not for me and rejected the whole idea.

At this point in my life, I thought religion and God were all wrapped up together. When I put religion on the back burner, I put God on the back burner, too. I began to ignore the idea of God or spiritual issues in thinking about what I would do with my life and how I would go about it.

My experience with cancer led me to reconsider religion and God. I also came to see there is a distinct difference between the two. I see God as the ever-present creative force in the universe, while religion reflects various interpretations of this creative force. The two are related, yet different.

Religion became a useful part of my process for bridging

the gap between infatuation with my mind and actual awareness of and contact with God.

I had spent a great deal of time focusing on mental processes. During this period, I also read a lot of interesting material, met many fascinating people, and had what I consider to be some rather remarkable experiences. For a while, I felt I was making good progress. Eventually I came to realize that I was mostly going around in circles within the limits of my own mind. In exploring ideas about God, I found I was limited by my old belief structures and by my "do it yourself" outlook. I was still trying to contact and commune with God from an independent point of view.

I studied a variety of spiritual figures and several religions but did not benefit much from these efforts. At the time it was not at all clear to me how one's mind, beliefs, God, spirituality, and religion fit together, or even if they did. However, my health was deteriorating and I felt my time in this dimension might be running out. If I was going to obtain help from religion, I was going to have to do it soon.

During this period, I was quite confused about the meaning of such terms as "God," "creation," "spirit," "life," and so on. I had read quite a few books that contained similar subject matter, but the meaning espoused by the various authors was not always the same. This led me into a lot more confusion, because I could not decide which one was "right."

In spite of my exploration of some eastern religions, I knew my religious knowledge was limited. But since time seemed to be growing short, I felt compelled to choose one religion quickly and delve into it deeply. I thought it best to pick a familiar religion and focus my energies on it. Since I am from Gainesville, Florida, and live in Chattanooga, Tennessee, it seemed reasonable to choose Christianity. Besides, I could not find anyone who had lived a life more exemplary than did Jesus. I needed a model, and he was the best one I could find. I also knew that Christ was a healer, and I needed and wanted his help.

I believe you will see that I was not rejecting the validity of other religions; instead, I was choosing the one I thought fit best into my mental, social, and cultural situation.

Settling on one religion enabled me to invest my time working for specific results, as opposed to spending my time—time I wasn't sure I had—in a long search for the "right" religion. I can tell you only about the fruits of Christianity, rather than about the many religious alternatives available. Please note, however, that Christianity produced such an abundance of fruit in my life that I have had no reason to search any further. I think this is a key point for weighing the value of any religion.

I feel awareness of God, contact or developing a relationship with God are basic purposes or objectives of many religions. Each religion also has its own distinctive content—beliefs, deities, rituals, and so forth. Each follower chooses to incorporate some, many, or all of these elements. In my view, such things serve to attune one's mind to God's "wavelength." In essence, I believe we make decisions with our minds that give permission for spiritual development. This facilitates the receipt of communion, guidance, blessings, forgiveness, or whatever is sought.

Another way to look at religion is to observe that it provides a way, or framework, for God's spirit to interact with us spiritually, mentally, and physically. As my beliefs changed, my mind became more open to spiritual possibilities. When my miraculous healing occurred on September 23, 1981, I experienced what I refer to as conscious awareness and interaction with the spiritual aspect of life, or God. This experience was the beginning of the death or decline of my infatuation with my own mind, and the emergence of my faith in spiritual things.

Religion helped me to reevaluate and redefine my concepts of God, the universe, and creation. Exploring these concepts led to changes in my life purpose and changes in my beliefs.

Many think of Christianity as a set of formal religious beliefs. Although Christianity certainly involves a set of beliefs, I now think of it more as a way of being and living defined by a new spiritual reality that guides me from within. In effect, my purposes in life are now defined by the spirit within rather than by my mind. My mind is now more involved as a recipient of beliefs rather than as the creator of beliefs, as was the case previously. I used religion as a tool to help me move toward deeper spirituality in my life. I was a "hoper" rather than a "believer" for a long time. It would have been a lot easier to have awakened one day with a new set of beliefs, but it just did not happen that way for me. I exerted a lot of effort over an extended period in cooperation with what I sensed was some form of unseen spiritual guidance.

In fact, I feel that the gradual change in my beliefs was orchestrated spiritually. I know I did not "figure things out" based on my old belief structures. In fact, the beliefs of my old self were very much against religion of any kind. Even so, time after time, that which I needed was provided, and often seemingly without rhyme or reason as far as I could tell.

I have found religion to be of continuing value in moving closer to God. In addition, my spiritual contact has grown deeper and more pervasive as I grasp more fully the tenets of the religion I have chosen to pursue. This is a continuing phenomenon. My understanding seems to grow as I study and apply my learnings to my life; yet, one of my primary realizations continues to be how little I know in relation to the wisdom of God. As I have grown in understanding, the significance of God has also grown in my awareness, and the very limited nature of human mental processes is more apparent as time passes. I have come to the conclusion that it is not necessary for me to fully understand God and his ways. In fact, I have found that I fare better in life by relying on God's guidance rather than on Reid's beliefs. I receive such guidance as I meditate after reading the Bible. Such insight usually comes in the form of the small inner voice of my spirit. On occasion, however, I have heard an audible voice. Typically, the guidance I receive is not in concert with human logic, but it is in accord with the teachings recorded in the Bible.

Comments on Letters Four, Five, and Six

Let's first address the idea that cancer has power. Just as Reid did, many cancer patients put great importance on the power of cancer itself. Some patients then feel compelled to find a treatment that sounds more powerful than the cancer; others withdraw from any effort to fight the cancer, thinking it so strong that of course it will overpower them.

Remind yourself that the predominant cultural beliefs about cancer are simply incorrect and not based in fact. You have learned that cancer is made up of weak, confused, deformed cells. When you take all the efforts you are making toward getting well again and put them up against the cancer cells in your body, cells that are weak by nature, then you might see that the power of cancer is small in comparison. In addition, if you believe that your family and friends are supporting your efforts, and/or if you believe that the force that created you supports your efforts, you have really empowered yourself to get well again. Remember that a primary problem with cancer is the unhealthy way you deal with the stresses of life, growing out of unhealthy beliefs that you can now change.

And even when you aren't consciously trying to influence your health, if you can just shift into neutral, you're helping yourself in every moment you do that. You don't have to make a gigantic effort in order to influence your health in a positive direction. You can take just a small step by relaxing now and then, or even by having a good time.

So keep all these things in mind when you think about the power of cancer, and reclaim some of that power for yourself today.

Exploring your beliefs about life will help you discover what you believe to be true about your illness on a deeper level. Your foundational beliefs influence all aspects of your life in a profound way.

Foundational beliefs are the beliefs that you hold about the nature of humanity, the nature of the world, the nature of the universe, the nature of the forces controlling the universe. Foundational beliefs are your beliefs about all there is, about how one aspect of life relates to any other, and how all aspects are interrelated.

There is no agreed-upon method for determining truth or accuracy of anyone's foundational beliefs; however, you now have some experience in determining the relative health value of beliefs by using Maultsby's five-question test we referred to in Chapter 4. (The first four questions apply to foundational beliefs.)

Many of you are probably still trying to identify your foundational beliefs, so I want to give you a simple exercise to get you started. Stop and ask yourself right now how you feel about your recovery: *Do you feel hopeful or hopeless?*

Let's look at what your feeling indicates about your beliefs. Hope reflects the belief that desirable things can happen to you, and that you can affect your life; hopelessness reflects the belief that your desires are unobtainable, and that no choices are available to you. In hopelessness there is an unconscious attitude of closure and rigidity; in hope there is openness and flexibility.

Can you see what your unconscious attitude about your illness reveals about your beliefs?

In working with foundational beliefs, the central issue often comes down to "Does the universe (or God) really care about me?" My suggestion is to practice sincerely thinking that it does. Affirm this on a regular basis and discover what happens.

Please be gentle with yourself in your explorations around foundational beliefs. In fact, this would be a good time to start being more gentle with yourself all the time.

Because spirituality, religion, and miracles are controversial issues for many people, I believe that timing is crucial in considering these matters. It is important to allow yourself to proceed in your own way, at your own pace. Because spiritual matters often arise indirectly, in surprising contexts—through exercise or nutrition or relationships, for example—I think it is unproductive to force yourself to explore them if you are not interested right now. Focus on whatever is important to you.

And for those of you who are interested in spiritual issues at this time, I suggest you embrace them with curiosity and excitement.

I have found that the healing process is not limited to any one group of people, to any one way of thinking, or to any one religion. People from all over the world, from a variety of religions with a wide range of beliefs and customs, have been miraculously cured. So have people who practice no religion but who are deeply spiritual. And so have people who have no concept of spirituality.

The ideas that Reid and I are presenting are not new. They've been around for a very long time, and they keep resurfacing in the work of one person after another. If you are strongly opposed to religious studies yet still yearn for some type of spiritual information, you will find an endless supply of reading material. (The recommended reading list at the end of this book will give you a start.) If a religious approach is uncomfortable for you, ask for recommendations from people who have an interest in spiritual matters but are not religious.

There are many other ways to explore spirituality. Just about any experience with nature is an opportunity to observe or feel part of the flow of life. Go camping. Plant a garden. Take a walk. Sit outdoors. Watch a sunset from your window.

Being absorbed in any creative activity can help you feel a spiritual connection with yourself and the world around you. Write, paint, draw, bake, sing, dance—do anything that stimulates joyful creativity.

Engaging in sports can also put you in touch with the flow of life. It's the feeling you get when you're in the moment and make that spectacular play, finding yourself moving just the right way at just the right time. Those moments can give you a sense of being in sync with the whole world.

Any experience of being connected with a force greater than yourself can make you conscious of the spiritual side of life. As you have more and more of these experiences, you begin to trust that connection and learn to use it as a resource for getting well.

_____ SEVEN

Doubt as a Process for Protecting Old Beliefs

Dear Friend,

For an extended period early in my cancer experience, I found myself wanting to believe various things and being very disturbed by recurring doubts. I saw such doubts as blocking my progress and became very frustrated as a result. This further accentuated the stress associated with an already difficult situation. Needless to say, I had plenty of doubt to work with.

In due course, I came to realize that my doubting mechanism was neither positive nor negative. Instead, it was and is a normal mental process that performs a very important function. As I observed myself, I realized that my doubts protected my existing belief structures. My mind automatically regarded my belief structures as valid. In my opinion, doubt does not evaluate beliefs, it protects them. It guards healthy beliefs as well as unhealthy ones.

Every time I read, observed, or experienced something that contradicted an existing belief structure, doubting thoughts arose in my mind. These thoughts questioned both the validity of the existing belief and the validity of the new interpretation or potential belief. However, I observed that at the outset of such a conflict, my doubts were heavily skewed in favor of my existing beliefs. I eventually realized that my doubts were generated by my existing belief structures and were biased accordingly. I discovered I had a strong tendency to reject anything that contradicted my existing beliefs.

Similar tendencies have been reported to me by other cancer patients. For example, a common hurdle is overcoming one's old beliefs about the "infallibility of doctors" and the doctors' ability to predict how long one will live. I found that it is impossible for any doctor to predict accurately how long I will live. In fact, I chose to believe that my doctors were not in charge of whether I would live or die—that was between me and God.

Here's how I handled statistics using my student point of view. Suppose a doctor said, "Nine out of ten people with characteristics such as those we now see in your body, Mr. Henson, live for six months or less." My thoughts would have been chosen along these lines:

> The doctor has stated statistical facts, but I am not like most people. I am me. Maybe the other people who had this disease did not want to make it. I do. Maybe the others did not work vigorously on their spiritual and mental well-being. I do. This doctor does not know about the spiritual/mental status of those who died or of those who lived.

I felt it was productive to hear what the doctor had to say about my illness, but I qualified his opinion by understanding that he had a limited viewpoint. I felt his statistics might not be relevant to me.

The doctor had focused on what he saw in my body at the time he observed it. He could only speculate as to what characteristics existed before or after this observation. Although such observations are often helpful, they can sometimes be misleading. The body is a dynamic mechanism that changes moment to moment.

Many healings occur in a way nobody understands.
People just get well for some reason beyond our human understanding.

In looking for alternative health care, the crucial issue for me centered around the power of medical procedures as compared with the power of mental/spiritual processes. Once again, I found the student approach immensely valuable. As a student, I could feel free to explore new thoughts, allowing my doubts to guide me. As I studied such phenomena as the placebo effect in medicine and the impact of hypnotic suggestion on the human body, and read case studies about the "will to live," I became less doubtful and more certain about the power of the mind and the spirit.

There is little question insofar as I am concerned that doubting is a very valuable and important mental function. If my mind had no doubting mechanism, I would be susceptible to every new idea to which I was exposed. My mental processes would continually flip-flop from one thing to the next. I would have no continuity in my life experience, and I would be unable to learn and retain things of value. The doubting mechanism protects my previous decisions regarding what is true and what is not. It enables me to build on what I have learned.

I have chosen many beliefs that were not helpful, although these beliefs had certainly seemed true at the time I accepted them and stored them in my subconscious mind. I had not previously seen a need to change those erroneous beliefs or even to review them consciously. Cancer gave me a compelling reason to observe my mind and its contents with considerable care. I saw my doubts as the fruit of the protective mechanism that guards beliefs, and this new perspective lowered my levels of fear, anxiety, and frustration as I explored new possibilities.

Comments on Letter Seven

As Reid points out, doubting can play an important role, protecting what you believe until you give any potential changes appropriate consideration. It can also be very useful in discovering what your beliefs are.

Try this simple exercise: Pretend that the universe is good, that there is a loving force that operates the universe, and that loving force is going to help you get well. Relax into this concept with a sense of hopefulness. Notice at what point doubt starts to creep into your mind. This will give you an experience of how Reid used doubt to point out his beliefs.

Now try the previous exercise in reverse: Pretend that the universe is evil, that it is operated by evil forces and those forces are not going to help you. Again, pay attention to the point at which doubt creeps into your mind.

Now pretend that one of these theories is closer to being correct than the other. Which would you rather believe? I'd say it would be much less stressful to practice believing in a good universe, wouldn't you? And now look at the emotions such beliefs produce.

Of course, defining the universe is not this simple, not this black or white. You don't have to sort out the whole universe, however, in order to move along with your work. For right now, try to discover just one unhealthy belief you are holding onto, and focus on changing that one belief. Every time you observe that you have a thought coming from the old belief, mentally say to yourself, "I doubt that because I really believe (your new belief) . . ." You can identify these unhealthy thoughts by being aware of the undesirable emotions or feelings they create.

The more aware you are that you are doubting your ability to get well, or doubting the ability of your treatment to work, the more aware you can become of the need to change your beliefs. Remember, your beliefs produce your feelings, so your unhealthy feelings point you to the unhealthy beliefs that you can consciously change with practice.

Once again, your response to the problem of continually doubting yourself can be much more important than the fact that you have doubts.

——————— *EIGHT*

A Miracle from Revelation and Repentance

Dear Friend,

I really can't explain how or why some people have profound spiritual experiences. It just happens for some reason, as it has for me several times over the years.

One such life-changing experience happened to me on September 23, 1981. Here is what occurred:

I was alone in my house, working on a process that a psychologist had suggested would be helpful in resolving some blaming issues related to my father. As the psychologist had instructed, I put an empty chair across from me and pictured my father sitting in it. I began telling him about something of great importance, when it suddenly occurred to me that all my life I had been very wrong in thinking he didn't love me. I began to cry, really sobbing deeply, with great remorse. It seemed to me there was error in the way God designed life in this world. I kept saying between sobs, "Why did it have to be this way?"

At some point, I entered a new state of consciousness that I can't begin to describe. My miraculous spiritual experience began. I did not see a vision. I heard no voices. Yet, words appeared, in a startling way, in my mind.

Here are the words that came to me that day:

IT DID NOT HAVE TO BE THIS WAY.
THIS IS THE PATH YOU CHOSE.
THE TEARS YOU ARE SHEDDING NOW
ARE THE TEARS I SHED FOR YOU WHILE
YOU WERE ON AN ERRANT COURSE.
THIS IS NOT THE ONLY RELATIONSHIP
YOU HAVE MISUNDERSTOOD.
I HAVE HEARD YOUR PRAYER FOR
HEALTH AND IT WILL BE ANSWERED IN
DUE COURSE.

Immediately doubt began to creep into my mind. I thought, "Is this a dream? Is my mind playing a trick on me? Is this actually real?" And while these doubts were still in the process of forming, they were stopped cold by these words, which were the same in nature and power as the proceeding ones:

THIS IS REAL!

Immediately all doubt was gone! I knew it was true! I knew this truth in a way that I had never known anything before. I couldn't explain it. I couldn't figure it out. But I did not need to. It was just true.

At this time in my illness, my blood counts were very low. I soon came down with a serious infection and had to be hospitalized. Several days later, my doctor came in and stood at the end of my bed, looking over my medical charts. Deep concern was written all over his face. With total confidence, I said, "Doc, you don't have to worry about me. I am going to be all right." He looked at me in a way that said, "If that's what he thinks, it's best for me to say as little as possible." So he said, "I hope so," and walked out.

That was in October 1981. On January 9, 1982, the same doctor called to advise me of the results of a recent blood test. He said, "Mr. Henson, I don't know what you have been doing, but I hope you'll tell me—your blood counts are better than mine!" I put down the phone and cried for a long, long time.

I will never forget my experience, the message I received on September 23, 1981. It is my most treasured memory. I don't need doctors, psychologists, preachers, friends, strangers, or anyone else to explain it to me. I know what happened! I was there! I lived this myself!

An experience of this type may not have come into your life up to this point. Yet, many people have had experiences along these lines. Many others have been inspired and given hope by similar events over the course of centuries.

I believe that by sharing this experience, others can benefit. This is my reason for sharing this experience with you. Who knows when something remarkable will happen to change your life? Just as cancer doesn't always happen to the other guy, neither do miracles occur only to other people.

I had no idea what was going to happen when I awakened on September 23, 1981. But I am glad I refused to give up when the going got tough on previous occasions. Look what I would have missed!

Comments on Letter Eight

First of all, let's consider what the word "miracle" means. The classic Webster's dictionary definition is that a miracle is an event or action that apparently contradicts known scientific laws and is hence thought to be due to supernatural causes, especially to an act of God. You can decide for yourself whether or not Reid's healing fits that definition.

To me, a miracle depends on one's point of view. One way I like to look at it is that everything in life is a miracle. It is a miracle that the earth exists. It is a miracle that we exist. The birth of a child is a miracle. The birth of an animal is a miracle. All these things are miraculous because we can't explain why they happen—we can partially explain how, but not why.

Some people choose to go to the other extreme and say that nothing is a miracle, that everything can be explained through current understanding.

Einstein once said that the truly unbelievable part of the universe is that we can comprehend it. To me, that indicates that he had had experiences of the interrelatedness of all things in the universe. I think many of us glimpse this insight when we have what we call "mountaintop" experiences—those times when we have a quiet knowing that all is well, or a certain peace of mind, or a feeling of being in the flow of things or being in harmony with all things around us.

In my opinion, those experiences are miraculous, and are of the same nature as Reid's deep knowing that God had communicated with him and that he would be well. To me, the fact that he had this understanding is as miraculous as the physical healing that followed.

I know that some of you will notice that the message from God contains a phrase that Reid himself often uses: "in due course." It has been my experience that when anyone receives a message from the creative forces of the universe, the message is in a language that the person can understand, with terms that mean the most to them, and with words that have the most powerful connections for them. If I get a message in my meditation, it's not in Russian, it's in English. That doesn't mean that God speaks in English, only that I hear in English, so that's how the message gets communicated to me.

But, just for the sake of argument, let's say the message that Reid got was not from God; suppose it came right out of his own subconscious. Well, what is the subconscious? No one really knows. Perhaps the subconscious is the link between each human being and the creative forces of the universe. And what if it was Reid's subconscious? Would that make any difference? Reid had an experience in which he became open to the mystery of life, in which he had a sense of knowing, an intense calm, a feeling that everything was going to be okay. On the deepest level of his being, the fear that had engulfed him was gone. In his heart and in his mind, he knew that he would be well. With that knowing came the appropriate physiological changes in his body.

If Reid had another episode of illness, it would not negate anything that had transpired up to this point. It would merely be another message, another lesson to learn.

I believe that Reid had a direct communication from God. At the same time, I believe that everything is part of God. If the message could somehow be proven to have come from Reid's subconscious, that wouldn't make any difference to me. If everything is part of God, then the subconscious is part of God. I myself have had two similar experiences, I know many others who have had them, and I

have read of hundreds more. I know we share in common
with Reid the profound feelings that come with the experience, the profound sense of understanding the connectedness of the universe and our place in it, and the wonderful
peace and joy that come with both.

But the experience does not have to be profound to be
valid. When you ask a question in meditation and get an
answer with a real gut feeling that the answer is right, you
have connected with the wisdom that resides within and
around you, just as Reid did. Appreciate that, like Reid,
you may doubt a message when it comes. Ask yourself, as
Reid did, if the information is true. If you know that it is,
then resolve to act on it and set a time frame for taking the
first step. Honor your feeling. Make decisions around it.
Make a definite plan and a definite commitment to implement the information. This will help you later if more
doubts occur, as they often do—especially if you need to
make changes in your life that trouble or inconvenience
others. You can go back to your decision and draw on your
memory of it, rather than dismissing the experience. Taking action is very important.

I believe that communication with the universe is possible and learnable. It is an active process, a process of
being open and exploring the imagination. It is acting on
what we understand now and staying open to the possibility
of understanding more later. Ask for understanding. Ask
for experiences like Reid's. Don't insist on a similar outcome, but have positive expectations about what may be
the outcome for you in your unique situation, in your
unique way.

——————— NINE

Finding a Purpose in Life

Dear Friend,

I believe my progress toward health accelerated considerably after I realized that my old purpose for living was not working for me and chose a new one.

For most of my life, I could not identify what my larger life purposes really were. Although there certainly were many things I wanted, there were also many contradictions, and I remember being frustrated by my inability to establish clear priorities.

I heard other people talk about personal objectives, but I never could seem to come to grips with such things myself. It seemed too complicated when I tried to think about it at the time. Now it seems clear that my real purpose then was to achieve what some people would call "success." I think it was necessary for me to prove to myself and others that I was a worthwhile person by achieving certain material things. I wanted lots of money, an important position with a good company, a nice house, fashionable clothes, a luxury car, and so on.

I eventually received just about all the material things I thought I wanted. However, once I had them, I realized they were of very little real value in enhancing my happiness in life. My experience with cancer brought this into sharp focus.

As a starting point in seeking a new life purpose, I decided I needed a broader perspective on life in general. I wanted to see how I fit into the overall scheme of things, thinking I might then discover what my true purpose should be. I put on my student hat and created a scenario that allowed me to look at life in a new way.

I decided to think of God as the owner of this planet, as a wealthy person who owns a very large estate. He invited me to be a guest on this estate for some reason, and I accepted the invitation, although I didn't know exactly what God had in mind for my visit.

Of course, there are other guests here on the estate as well. They seem to be pretty much in the same situation as I am. They, too, are invited guests. They didn't bring anything with them, and they take nothing when they leave. Some stay longer than others.

The owner has provided well for me and the other guests. He gives us air to breathe, water to drink, food to eat, clothing, shelter, and other guests for company. He is obviously very generous, so in view of his generosity, it seems appropriate to try to be a good guest.

It also seems obvious that a good guest should at least try not to mess up this beautiful estate. I can use it freely, but I should try to leave it as I found it after providing for my needs. I should not be wasteful in using the resources of the estate, nor should I defile its natural beauty. In short, I should be considerate in dealing with the owner's property.

It also seems appropriate for me to be kind and considerate to the other guests, and not to interfere with their enjoyment. They have the same relationship with the owner as I do, so I am certainly in no position to tell them what to do—especially since I really don't know what to do myself. But I can certainly conduct myself so as not to harm them or interfere with their activities.

I decided that I wanted to conduct myself in a manner similar to that of the owner. He is kind and considerate in providing for my needs and those of the other guests. He has obviously given us lots of freedom.

The estate is magnificent in its design, vastly complicated and completely interdependent. Every aspect of the estate interacts with every other aspect, including the guests. The whole thing seems to be alive and responsive to the slightest change, no matter how small. It seems some wisdom is always at work in responding to every change. Also, the wisdom of the owner seems to prevail, as the estate adapts to every disruption and continually moves toward balance, which entails complete harmony.

This experiment in looking at life on earth from a new point of view did not, and has not, revealed God's purpose to me, but it has enabled me to see God, myself, and others in a balanced and helpful way. Not only am I a student of life, I am an invited guest who is here to serve God's purposes rather than my own. Yet by serving harmoniously with the creator, my own life experience is also maximized.

In observing how my mind works, I eventually came to understand that it is a mechanism designed to serve the purposes I choose. Once I choose a purpose, the automaticity of my mind takes over. All its functions are then designed to activate or manifest the purpose chosen. My mind is highly selective in this regard. After I set forth a purpose, my mind is then focused on the things that can contribute in some way to accomplish it. My mind does not give equal consideration to all the events of my life. It considers some more important than others. In fact, it treats with importance only those things that are relevant to the accomplishment of my purpose. Other events are noted and stored subconsciously, but are not given the same conscious attention.

For example, if I decide to go to Atlanta, my mind automatically excludes any information it has about New York, Chicago, Los Angeles, and so on. Once I choose Atlanta, other possible destinations are not relevant. My mind presents only the questions related to the destination I have chosen: When will I go to Atlanta? How will I get there? Do I want to drive or fly? Where do I want to stay?

Similarly, once we determine a purpose in life, our mind presents only the information relevant to that purpose. When my purpose was to achieve success, I tended to see everything that happened in light of that purpose. When my purpose became serving God and his creation, I began to make some real headway in my search for health. I also noted that my life seemed to be moving toward greater harmony in other areas.

My purpose became further defined as the result of an experience I had when I was near death in the hospital. Looking back over my life, I felt as though I were literally dividing in two: My errant part separated completely from the part that was intact and pure. It became quite obvious to me that the really important things in our lives are the unselfish things we do in a loving way for other people. Even the smallest acts done unselfishly and with love have a profound effect on the universe. I believe they are indelibly recorded to our credit in some way. Material things are relevant only in this physical dimension. The most valuable gift may be one that costs no money at all. Intent is the key issue.

Although my perception of my life's purpose continues to change, the way I communicate it at this time is to say that I want to express the love of God in whatever I am doing, and that I want to choose to do things that are harmonious with God and his creation.

It took a long time for me to come to grips with the

awesome importance of choosing a worthwhile purpose for my life. It was indeed a choice with vast consequences.

The turning point for me came when I began thinking about what I could be doing with the opportunities God was giving me in this dimension. Even small changes in my purpose seemed to have profound long-term ramifications. As I defined my purpose more clearly, I began to see and experience life differently.

Comments on Letter Nine

In the past, Reid had seen himself more or less as the center of his universe, with all things available to serve his purpose of achieving success. Once he began to think of himself as a guest on the planet, he was no longer the center of the universe, but rather a part of it. This gave him a new perspective. He could see how his day-to-day activities fit into a bigger picture; he began to understand his purpose within the overall scheme of things. He started by just trying to be a good guest on the planet, and in doing so he took the first step in clarifying his purpose as serving life, or God.

If you are trying to discover your purpose and have felt lost in this pursuit, I suggest that you follow Reid's example. Try looking at yourself as a guest here on the planet. What contribution can you offer? What unique talents do you have? How are you using them to make your life happy and fulfilled?

In examining your purpose, one important area to look at is what you do for others and how that affects what you do for yourself. Remember Reid's experience with the halfway house and with his business—he was spending a lot of time helping others when he needed to focus on himself. Once Reid regained his health, he was able to make many wonderful contributions, including sharing what he learned from his cancer experiences.

I am not saying that you can't make taking care of others part of your purpose in life right now. If it gives you joy, go in that direction. Just don't do it to the detriment of your health.

Perhaps you have always taken care of others, but those others are no longer around to be taken care of—your kids have grown up and moved away, or your spouse died, or you took care of your parents and they have now died. Is serving in this role still important to you? Consider new ways to fulfill your purpose. There are so many ways to do this—volunteer your time at a soup kitchen for the homeless; get your church to put you in touch with someone who is homebound and correspond with or regularly call that person; volunteer to baby-sit for a neighbor; donate your time and skills to a recycling center—the possibilities are endless.

Remember that your purpose in life can change. While your purpose in life may once have been to take care of others, perhaps it is time to let that role go and now let others take care of you.

If you are having a hard time defining your purpose in life, it may help to bring your focus down. Define your purpose for today. Your purpose today may be to get some rest. Your purpose today may be to enhance your treatment through meditation. Your purpose today may be to write a letter to your granddaughter. Once you get comfortable focusing on a purpose every day, you can do more work on defining your purpose in life. How does getting some rest today or enhancing your treatment through meditation tie into a large purpose? It could be the first step in defining your purpose as using your cancer experience to gain a new appreciation for life. How does writing a letter to your granddaughter tie into a larger purpose? You could see it as the first step in defining your purpose to be passing on your wisdom to your family so that their lives will be enriched. These are just a few examples that I hope will give you some help in clarifying purpose.

Another way to approach your purpose is simply to look at what you are most interested in or where your talents lie. If you love to cook, maybe your purpose lies in using that skill. If you're a good carpenter, maybe your purpose involves carpentry. If you're a computer whiz, maybe your purpose has something to do with computers.

Take a few minutes to write down what you are good at and how you can use your skills to serve yourself or someone else. In either case, like Reid, you will be serving life. Remember to consult your inner wisdom also for help in clarifying effective areas of service for you.

——————— *TEN*

Rekindling the Will to Live

Dear Friend,

I believe there is a definite correlation between my will to live and my health. I also think that my will to live is affected by my thoughts and beliefs, as well as by my enjoyment of life. In my view, all of these rest on, or arise out of, my beliefs about God, which define the boundaries within which I perceive my life experiences. I can't prove this to anyone; I just know it's true for me.

As you may recall, prior to the diagnosis of cancer I seemed to be having one personal problem after another— the death of a son at birth, divorce, my son's addiction to drugs. I saw no end to these difficulties, and I was very discouraged about life in general. I had less and less confidence that I could cope successfully with the difficult problems I was encountering. A feeling of helplessness had emerged in my life, and with it, a feeling of hopelessness.

It is important to understand that I did not consciously wish to die, even though my subconscious beliefs about guilt and punishment indicated that I did not deserve to live. In fact, I thought I was going to live for a long time. I was in top physical condition, or so it appeared. I exercised vigorously and regularly. I didn't smoke. There were a few bright spots in my life, but only a few. The preponderance of my life had evolved into work, work, work. I now realize my career was an escape mechanism for me. When I filled my mind with work-related topics, I didn't have to think about my personal problems.

I had very little experience in dealing with my personal problems. I usually just ignored them. In retrospect, I can see that I tended to focus on the issues I felt competent to handle—those of a business nature. Postponing dealing with personal problems sounded very reasonable to me at the time. Nevertheless, this approach didn't work in the long run.

It seems to me that deep dissatisfaction with life (often called depression, among other things) causes some subconscious "switches" to be flipped that prepare the body for death—which releases the person from the very troubling circumstances encountered in this dimension. My normal bodily functions were altered. Significant changes became evident over a period of time, with the eventual diagnosis of cancer.

From my perspective as a student of life, I began to take a hard look at what my life had been. I could then see that for me, cancer was a red flag, indicating that changes in my life were indeed necessary. I realized that one of the positive things about my illness was that I now had time off from work to devote to making changes. And I had a compelling reason to start working on personal issues immediately—I was told I was going to die.

In many ways, I see my cancer as the natural result of my own errant purposes and misunderstandings about life. These, of course, gave rise to problems that, in turn, produced a continuing dose of stress and anxiety. My new perspective as a student of life led to new ideas about my purpose in life, as well as to many changes in my beliefs.

At one time, I had found it frightening to explore ideas that were "on the fringe," outside what was familiar to me. I now realize I was afraid I would learn that some of my existing beliefs were in error. This would have been disquieting to me in view of the ideas I held at the time, which included the need to be right about everything. However, as a student of life, I could comfortably explore ideas, materials, and dimensions that I had never considered before. As I got more practice as a student, I found that this type of mental and spiritual exploration was inspiring, joyful, and very valuable.

As I made progress in my student role, many of my previous errors seemed to be corrected almost without struggle. It felt more like unlearning than learning. As I began to peel away the layers of confusion, my new focus on living in harmony with God and his creation became clearer. As my level of understanding improved, life became more wondrous and more beautiful. At some point, I began to experience love for God, for life, and for my fellow man. Although I still find it easy to drift back into old patterns, love freed me from my traditional worldly point of view and gave me a totally new perspective, from which I gained joy and hope. My will to live seemed to increase in direct proportion.

I decided that whether I lived long or not, I certainly would live the days left more enjoyably than I had in the past. My will to live got stronger day by day. I have lived a lot longer than anyone expected, and I feel better now than I have in years.

As my concern for other patients grew, I decided to conduct myself with the recognition that others could learn from my experiences. I did not see myself as responsible for others. Instead, I saw my illness as an opportunity for me to learn and thereby to offer a helpful example. As I have said, this may seem to be a minor point, but it was very important to me. Without realizing it, I gave myself a mission that exceeded my own selfish interests. On quite a few occasions, when the chips were down, I had something extra to draw from—a purpose beyond myself, a reason to go on. It made a significant difference to me on repeated occasions. I felt my path had been much too difficult and painful to waste. I refused to give up no matter how bleak the outlook. Somehow, I felt I would live and use what I had learned to be of help to others. As a consequence of these experiences, I believe a wholesome purpose in life is inexorably interwoven with the will to live.

_____ *ELEVEN*

The Mind–Body Relationship

Dear Friend,

In our Western culture, physicians are trained to associate names of diseases with particular groups of physical characteristics. This helps them identify an illness so that effective treatment can be given, based on experience with many similar cases. This makes sense to me. When I work out a business problem, I also identify and define it, then I look for the origin so that effective solutions can be developed and implemented.

The medical community was very honest in stating that they did not have a solution to my problem. I had a group of physical characteristics labeled cancer. More specifically, the label was hairy-cell leukemia. There was no known effective treatment for this problem at the time. Thus, the illness was terminal, as far as the medical establishment was concerned.

My doctors paid very little attention to my mental condition and none whatever to my spiritual state. I know this is not the role of the physician in our culture, but I believe they ignored a vast part of the human equation in their analysis of my illness. I believe this is a major weakness in our current health care system.

Since traditional medicine offered no hope of recovery, it was readily apparent to me that I would have to go farther on my own in evaluating my illness, finding its source, and then doing something about it. Of course, I was afraid that my efforts might not work, but if I wanted to survive, it seemed to me that there simply was no alternative to trying. Otherwise, my physician's grim prognostication would become a reality.

During this time, I found it highly productive to think of my inner processes as a network of interdependent physical, mental, and spiritual systems, each with distinct functions and characteristics. In this way, I was able to isolate each part for observation and study. Gradually, a seemingly sensible overall picture emerged.

One of the things I discovered about myself was that whenever I felt stress, I also had some sort of internal conflict going on. At such times, there was a difference between what was happening and what I thought should be happening. I was spending a lot of time struggling to get from where I was in any given moment to where I wanted to be. I realized this was stressful and therefore detrimental to my health. I gradually found it more productive to put on my "student hat" and see what I could learn from each experience.

Let me give you an example. I have had lower back pain off and on for years, so I am quick to notice any changes in that area of my body. Several years ago, I was enjoying a winter ski trip in Colorado. I got off-track somehow and found myself at the top of a very steep and difficult ski run. As soon as I thought about the possibility of falling and hurting myself, I noticed tension in my lower back muscles, followed by pain. Finally, I skied down the steep slope and got in line again at the ski lift at the bottom. While standing there, I noticed the tension and pain were gone. This indicated to me that there is some correlation between fearful thoughts and neuro-muscular tension.

My body had been in a state of chemical imbalance resulting from my mental processes. This adaptation by my body seemed normal, considering the circumstances perceived by my mind. But I could have changed those mental processes. If I had been wearing my student hat, I could have chosen to enjoy a difficult skiing experience by putting faith in life, in God, and in myself. There was an excellent chance I could make it down the slope without injury, but I didn't look at it that way. If I had, I might well have skied without tension and anxiety, and with much greater enjoyment.

Let me give you another example, one that may seem more familiar to you as a cancer patient.

Since there was no effective treatment for my physical condition in 1979, my doctors asked me to try a variety of "experiments." One particular drug they wanted me to try killed cancer cells, but it killed healthy cells as well. It was very dangerous. My doctors believed the drug could help me, but they also admitted that it could do a lot of damage. I found I was unable to look at this drug as a "helper." I viewed it as pure poison, and I found it very stressful to take the pills. My health continued to decline.

I knew my attitude was not helpful, so I started working on it through self-hypnosis, prayer, and other tools. In time, my outlook changed significantly. I was eventually able to focus more of my attention on the positive aspects of the drug, and I began to take it with relative ease. My view shifted from fear and foreboding to something between neutral and hopeful expectation. Guess what? My physical condition began to improve. I was amazed at how a small shift in my point of view seemed to produce remarkable results.

Here's another example. As my red blood counts went down, I found it more and more difficult to climb the stairs to my bedroom. I unconsciously began to use the stairs as an index of my health. If the stairs were difficult to climb, I would think I was getting worse. Then I began to dread going upstairs because I didn't want the "bad news."

Then I put on my student hat. Using what I had learned about how my mind works, I began to experiment with disagreeing with these negative thoughts. After all, I had no meter on my body to measure how difficult climbing the stairs really was. Perhaps my mind was interpreting my body's functions incorrectly due to some negative subconscious beliefs. As I began to be more conscious that I might be deliberately undermining my own strength with negative thoughts, these thoughts seemed to lose much of their power. I soon found climbing the stairs less of a struggle and a lot less depressing.

In time, some of the seemingly small changes I made in my thinking seemed to allow me to receive more profound spiritual ideas and assistance. Together, my spiritual and mental aspects seemed to be getting stronger, and I believe the two enhanced my physical well-being in ways I do not fully understand.

I want to point out that there is a difference between mental thoughts and spiritual input. I was familiar with the thoughts produced by my mind, since I had been dealing with such things all my life. But spiritual input felt quite different. I now believe it is profoundly different in origin and content.

To help myself distinguish between mental and spiritual processes, I began to assume that all negative thoughts about my future health came from my mind—from erroneous, subconscious belief structures. These thoughts often came with a feeling of fear. As I questioned these negative thoughts from my student perspective, I found their impact diminished over time.

I believed that by dampening the impact of my mind's negative thoughts, I would somehow enhance the likelihood that God would accomplish the changes I needed in due course. In other words, if I removed the obstacle of negative thoughts, God's love would come through and manifest in healthy changes. Such thoughts gave me comfort.

I have found that if I consistently observe whatever I am doing, I then have the power to choose the point of view I want to use in that moment. I have experienced a strong correlation between my mental outlook and my physical state. I now refer to this interaction as "adaptation," and I see it as a normal process. It seems that our spiritual/mental aspects are constantly changing, and that the manifestations of these changes are visible in our bodies; some thoughts, such as fear, produce immediate changes, while other changes occur over longer periods of time. I think this is a very exciting concept because, on a broad scale, it means that if a negative mind-set contributes to illness, then maybe a positive one can help produce health.

Comments on Letters Ten and Eleven

As it did with Reid, the threat of death frequently makes people start paying attention to their lives. Changes result and those changes are built upon, with changes in foundational beliefs having a profound effect on the life of the individual. I often see patients emerge from illness with very different priorities than the ones they took into it.

Let's look at some healthy foundational beliefs that could make a profound difference in your life:

- Humans are good by nature. I am good by nature.
- The nature of the universe is good, loving, and orderly.
- The creative force of the universe is loving and all-knowing, knowing each of us individually better than we know ourselves, and caring for us and loving us more than we love ourselves.
- Life is a loving teacher, and we are here to learn who we are.
- Illness is a negative feedback experience that brings us back to our nature.
- Health, happiness, joy, deep fulfillment, and love are positive feedback that we are moving in the direction of who we are and are connected with our purpose.
- Death is the end of this existence, as birth is the beginning. Our essence (or consciousness or soul) continues after death, and that existence is desirable.
- Our own unique individual unfolding is built into each of us. We are directed by desire, passion, joy, love,

happiness, and fulfillment, and we are guided by the forces that created us.

What you believe about life influences your will to live. If you have terrible thoughts about life, why would you want to live, other than to avoid whatever you fear about death? Whereas, if you love life and believe life to be good and worthwhile, of course you want to live. If you have healthy beliefs about death, you will have less fear of dying, and more of your energy will be available for living life today.

Remember that prior to the diagnosis of cancer, Reid's life had become burdensome and he felt there was no way out from under all his problems. But in facing his life problems, Reid found the solution to his illness. He found life to be good again, and he returned to a state of good health.

As you study yourself, observing your thoughts and feelings, it is important to use your new awareness and understanding of life in a way that increases your will to live:

• Consult your goals listed under "Play" on your two-year health plan. This week, focus on meeting those goals or experiment with going beyond them. Enjoy your life and observe, from the student point of view, how this enjoyment influences your will to live.

• Using your journal to record your thoughts, write down one problem in life that was difficult for you but that you overcame and learned from. How can you translate what you learned from that experience to your experience with getting well?

Healing is a creative process. Be sensitive to your needs and aware of your strengths. Improvise and draw on your knowledge and experience as each situation in life unfolds. If you have problems that seem beyond your own resources, ask for help. I can't emphasize this enough. Help is all around you, no matter what problems you have with your illness or your life. Ask for physical, mental, and spiritual help—not just from professionals—when you need it. Call on your support team when you need them. Rely on your support person. Be open to every resource that will move you toward health. As you become more confident of your ability to get help from both your inner processes and outside sources, you will naturally feel less burdened; you will have a greater desire to be a part of life and life's activities.

Now let's address the mind–body relationship and work further with that concept. It's hard to want to live if you don't believe you can live. Believing you can live is strengthened by believing you can influence your body and by trusting in your body's ability to heal itself.

If I have a cold, the problem is not that some virus entered my body and attacked me and overpowered my immune system. The problem is that I did something to weaken my immune system, which would normally have taken care of the virus without my getting a cold. If I look back, I always see that prior to getting the cold, I was under an unusual amount of stress, or I was experiencing negative emotions in an extreme way or for an extended period of time.

Rather than trying to control the cancer itself, I want you to try to influence your symptoms just as I looked for the source of my cold. Whenever a symptom flares up, look back a few days and review what was going on in your life. Recall any negative emotions you've experienced, and record this information in your journal. After doing this several times, try to note any patterns. For example, do you find that when you are scheduled for treatment, you develop symptoms that prevent you from having the treatment as scheduled? If so, work on your beliefs and emotions about treatment. Take appropriate actions such as changing your beliefs in a healthy direction and discussing your reactions with your doctor or therapist. This will begin to address your symptoms at their source.

Remember that the body is a marvelous organism that heals itself under normal circumstances. To move toward health, look at what you are doing to interfere with that process, and stop interfering. You can get out of the way by shifting to a neutral state emotionally. Continue to attempt to do that by meditating regularly.

_____ TWELVE

Healing Important Relationships

Dear Friend,

I want to make it very clear that I have the highest regard
for my dad. He died in 1983 at eighty-six years of age. But
for the first forty-two years of my life, my relationship with
my father was what I would describe as troubled, at best.

If my father ever told me he loved me, I am completely
unaware of it. Insofar as I know, he never once put his arms
around me, never hugged me, and words of encouragement
or support were either very few or non-existent. I felt
unloved and unwanted by him. My relationship with my
mother was very different. She was full of loving ways and
encouragement. I do not say this to indicate that one was
better than the other, but rather to highlight the differences that I perceived.

Although my relationship with my dad troubled me
greatly, especially in my youth, I just didn't feel that it was
something I could talk about with him. In fact, I felt
uncomfortable talking with him about most things. At
some point, I just decided to accept things as they were
with my dad and get on with my life.

By the time cancer entered my life in 1979, I had
developed the habit of ignoring this troublesome relationship. I had lived far from my parents' home for roughly
twenty years, and these old feelings surfaced only on my

infrequent visits. I guess the limited contact and years of ignoring the issue dulled its significance in my perception.

In any case, the psychologist assisting me soon realized that I had a long-standing problem of considerable importance that I no longer recognized as such. He quickly brought this issue between my dad and me to my attention. Even then I did not feel it was significant.

Since many of my thoughts and feelings had been ignored for such a long time, it took considerable effort to recall the specifics of our relationship. After much work, I finally realized that my dad really did love me but showed his love by providing for my needs. I was given food, clothing, and shelter, and this was his way of showing he truly cared for me. For some reason, I just hadn't been able to see this up to the time of my illness. I believe part of the problem stemmed from the fact that my friends' fathers seemed to behave quite differently. I suppose my expectations for my father just didn't match his way of expressing love.

I now realize that I misunderstood my Heavenly Father in a similar way. He has provided for my needs in his way. Unfortunately, for too many years, I wanted God to provide for my desires in my way and on my schedule. Since things hadn't worked out my way, I felt that both God and the world were often against me. I couldn't see that God was providing for me in a very loving way, and I misunderstood him just as I had misunderstood my father on earth. In fact the problem was in my way of responding, not in their way of providing.

The thing that once again strikes home as I write about all of this is the profound effect a small change in perception had on my life. By focusing on an old problem from a different perspective, I found that my interpretation of the present changed as well. Once again, I was able to obtain considerable relief from the burdens of guilt and blame that

I had felt for many years. This took away much pain and contributed to my enjoying life in a way that I never had before.

You may recall that just moments prior to my miraculous healing in 1981, I was doing a mental exercise to help me with my relationship with my father. You might like to reread the details in the letter about the miracle, but for now, I want to emphasize that I sometimes found I really needed to work on things that I thought had no current importance. I had suppressed some major problems for so long that my mind had developed habits designed to ignore or minimize them. But I found that such issues had not gone away; they still distorted my perception of life. My habit of overlooking these issues may have given me comfort at some point, but it became destructive over time.

I now believe that I was greatly helped by my decision to work with a psychologist. Many psychologists have experience in helping people deal with and heal old emotional scars—a process that proved to be vitally important to me. Despite my initial doubts, I wanted to use every resource available, and the only way I could determine whether or not a resource was useful was to give it a fair trial. The work I did with the psychologist was of great value in many ways, including the healing of my relationship with my father—on earth and in heaven.

Comments on Letter Twelve

A troublesome relationship with one or both parents is a common experience among cancer patients, so I encourage you to look at this issue closely. The specific issue of harboring resentments is very important to evaluate and resolve. You can do this work, as Reid did, even if your parents are dead. You can do it whether or not you are in contact with your parents. Our focus is on changing *your* beliefs and the feelings they create.

I sometimes find that a patient does not want to forgive a parent, because he or she feels so wronged. They may believe that to forgive their parent condones the cruelty or injustice they experienced. But you can acknowledge your hurt and still forgive. Remember that you are not doing this for your parents. You are doing it for yourself. Through forgiveness, you release the pain and anger that keep you tied to the past.

One good tool for changing your beliefs about your parents is to appreciate that we all do the best we can with the understanding and feelings we have at the time. We can use this tool to forgive our parents and others, and perhaps more importantly, to forgive ourselves. When our patients acknowledge to themselves that their parents did the best they could, they often find that their day-to-day relationships begin to get easier. Sometimes nothing is said—there is no big reconciliation—yet the shift in attitude brings about a real change.

But you can forgive even if your relationship continues to be difficult. One of our patients with advanced breast cancer had always had a poor relationship with her mother, who was a very negative and critical person. After she was diagnosed, her mother called regularly with messages of anxiety and gloom; she clearly believed her daughter was dying. Once the daughter recognized that her mother was doing the best she could coming from her life experiences and beliefs, she also recognized that she had a right to refuse these messages. She told her mother that she would get in touch if she wanted to talk, but that otherwise she couldn't take her calls while she was doing her healing work. Six years later, she is free of disease and again in communication with her mother—but on a very different basis.

The result of forgiving can move you toward health, so I urge you to do the work if for no other reason. However, I think you will find that forgiveness has a far-reaching impact in many other areas of your life as well.

——————— *THIRTEEN*

Dealing with Family and Friends

Dear Friend,

I came to realize that a life-threatening illness has a wide-spread impact on a lot of people. It can be an opportunity for all concerned. Most people will give some thought to why this has happened and how they would react if it happened to them. I decided that my conduct could be an inspiration and a source of guidance for others, even if I struggled greatly. Eventually I realized I had given myself a valuable gift in the form of a purpose that extended beyond myself. I was able to draw on this purpose later to do things I don't think I would have been able to do if I had been thinking only of myself. This is a sobering realization as I look back on my experience.

It would have been easy to throw in the towel and give up on many occasions. However, as I thought about the pain and difficulties I had already been through, as well as the remarkable experiences that had come my way, I just refused to give up. I hoped that someday my journey could be helpful to others in some way.

As my illness progressed, I soon recognized that other people simply could not grasp my point of view about life. They were not facing death and I was. There was no way for them to accurately imagine something they had not dealt with and didn't want to face. I later realized that most of them cared deeply but didn't know how to help me. Their intentions were good, but they were lacking in experience and skills. Also, their emotions were so strong that I would wind up helping some of the people who wanted to help me. I don't feel critical toward others in this respect, it's just that most were more in a position to receive help than to give it, since they had never been so close to a life-threatening illness before. I concluded that friends and relatives could best provide love, companionship, and support. Of course, some were helpful in other ways.

I was very lucky in that my family and friends never insisted on my following their advice. I didn't realize how important this was until I talked with others going through a life-threatening illness who were not so fortunate.

I don't claim to know anything about family psychology, but it does appear to me that often there is a dominant person in the family. Sometimes the husband is dominant, sometimes the wife, sometimes even a child. If the sick person is not the dominant family member, there is often an inclination for the dominant member to tell the sick person what to do. This can be a huge obstacle to healing. In the first place, the dominant person is often scared. He or she may feel responsible for the sick person and for solving a health problem that he or she may not even think is solvable. Seeing failure and death coming down the path, a dominant person often becomes even more domineering in attempting to stop the progress of the illness.

Based on what I have learned in talking with other cancer patients, this situation is fairly common. It seems to help if patients first accept the fact that they themselves are the key to finding a resolution to their own health problems, regardless of who usually makes the decisions in the family. I believe it also helps if patients make it clear that other people will have a role in their recovery, but that they, the sick person, must be in charge inasmuch as they are the only ones who truly know what is going on with them spiritually, mentally, and physically. As a patient, you may want to let people know that you appreciate their support and encouragement, but that their advice is best heard when presented as suggestions or ideas for consideration. This is what I did. You may have another approach to handling your family. My objective was to help all concerned better understand how they could be genuinely helpful.

_____ FOURTEEN

The Family as a Support System

Dear Friend,

One of the things I found helpful in my cancer experience was to organize a family support system, with various members assigned a role that would help me reach my objective—getting well again. My experience indicates that there is a wide variety of roles to be played, according to the circumstances and personalities involved. You will do well to realize that each person brings his or her own set of beliefs, biases, misunderstandings, etc., to the role they are asked to play. This does not have to be a formal process. No job descriptions are required. However, a healthy discussion is quite helpful.

Sometimes the life-threatening illness itself will precipitate difficult issues for members of the family. Some may find these so difficult that they are unable to play their support roles effectively for some period of time. They need time to learn, and they need the understanding and compassion of other family members. Also, some may find it difficult to play an assigned role. This is often the case with the dominant family member, who wants to be in charge but really can't because the situation is often far beyond his or her control.

It is important for everyone in the family support system to realize that their efforts are most helpful when they support the choices of the sick person. You may want to ask one person to play the role of senior support person, someone who would make decisions for you if you reach a point when you are no longer able, or no longer desire, to do so. Realize that this is a very difficult responsibility and that it can give rise to significant guilt when the results of the decisions the support person makes do not unfold as he or she or other family members wanted or expected. Senior or primary support persons have to be prepared for such situations, to know that they can only do what they think is reasonable under the circumstances and that the rest is in God's hands.

If the person experiencing illness is married, the senior support person is often the spouse. If not, it could be any willing person chosen by the patient. This person will likely spend more time with the sick person and be more deeply involved than any other member of the family support system.

It is important for this person to realize that he or she can't get well for the sick person, no matter how hard the effort made. From my experience, I feel it is imperative that the right to choose clearly rest with the sick person as long as he or she is able. I know that this can be extremely difficult if the ill person surrenders his or her will to live. Under such conditions, I believe family members should feel free to offer information, insight, and encouragement. But nobody really knows how much the patient has endured or is willing to endure in the future.

I have been close to death on several occasions. I definitely did not want anyone making any key decisions for me as long as I was able to make them for myself. I know that if I become unable to make my own decisions, I will appreciate the assistance of others whom I have asked to play this role, but not until then.

Life itself is terminal from a physical standpoint, as far as I know. People often find this reality difficult to face. Yet it is a reality in our world, and every member of every family has to face that reality sooner or later.

I believe that it is especially helpful to the person experiencing illness if the family members and other supporters can view the illness as an opportunity to learn more about life and to strengthen the family. I believe that a key point is the realization that the family can work as a team when willing to do so. In fact, I know families who have found it quite invigorating to realize that none of them need to face the challenges of life alone. What the family does now for you can easily be seen as being done for each of them when the need arises. All can feel renewed comfort and strength as a result.

_____ *FIFTEEN*

The Primary Support Person

Dear Friend,

Early in my illness, I did not make good use of my family resources and thereby placed an even greater burden on my wife, Jana. Fortunately, she proved to be a tremendously strong primary support person. A person with less strength might well have faltered under the pressure. Thus, I suggest making good use of other resources in order to alleviate unnecessary pressure on any one individual.

Repeatedly, I was forced to delegate many things to Jana because I was too sick to do them myself. At other times, I wanted to focus all my energies on getting well, so once again she was indispensable. In a way, I suspect the role of the primary support person may be more difficult than being sick. I had to face the fear of death, the pain of treatment, the sickness that goes along with it, and a lot more. As I saw it, the only other choice at the time was to give up and die. On the other hand, Jana felt fine, but she had to spend many of her days in a hospital full of very sick people. She was faced with many unpleasant duties, including decisions that had a direct bearing on my survival. She also dealt with a great deal of fear, anxiety, uncertainty, potential guilt, and so forth. It was a very difficult role to play, but she played it superbly.

My wife had a distinct tendency to put my needs before

her own. She felt she should make this sacrifice to help me get through a difficult period. This sounds logical, but the problem is that nobody knows how long these periods of critical illness will last. When I was in the hospital in Dallas, I sensed several times that her physical and mental resources were wearing thin. I insisted that she go home to Chattanooga for a week or two to "recharge her batteries." Our home, friends, familiar surroundings, pets, and so forth seemed to do wonders for her morale. She always came back with a much improved outlook, which made our relationship more enjoyable.

This reminds me of something I used to tell plant managers who tended to be workaholics. They felt they had to work long hours to do their jobs properly and to provide for their families. I pointed out that if they didn't take care of themselves first, they would neither be able to do their jobs nor provide for their families. Some thought that taking care of their own needs first was selfish. Nevertheless, if a person doesn't take care of his or her own needs, he or she certainly won't be able to help others in a quality way over an extended period of time. I have found that serious illness in the family is more likely to increase the spouse's needs than to reduce them.

Even though I reminded Jana of this periodically, I sometimes had to insist on her taking care of herself. In fact, her efforts occasionally became counterproductive when she did not provide for her own needs in a timely manner. Her dedication to my well-being was so strong that it backfired for both of us on several occasions.

Other members of the support group may become needy as well. A life-threatening illness presents each member of the family with a very visible reminder of the fact that physical life in this world does not go on forever. Those who have not previously come to grips with their own mortality can find this situation very difficult. (It seems that this applies to most people in our society.) Some find that their emotions get completely out of hand and are soon exhibiting behavior that is detrimental to the efforts of the family support group. Here again, they must make arrangements to help themselves before they can contribute in a productive way to the well-being of others.

I think it is important to be alert for such developments. A healthy support person can be a huge asset, but a needy support person can add to the already heavy burden of the illness. You certainly don't need something else to divert your attention and drain your energies. In short, give your support members permission to take care of their own needs, and if that is not enough, insist that they do so in order to avoid the potential drain on your own strength.

Of course, there were times when I simply did not feel up to dealing with my own support system. My wife did this for me when I was unable or unwilling to do it for myself. In some cases, I chose to ask her to do things I really could have done myself but felt my energy was better invested in activities more directly related to my health.

Jana followed up with hospital dietitians to ensure I got the foods I requested. She kept nurses out of my room while I was taking naps. She screened my telephone calls when I didn't feel like taking them myself. She asked hospital personnel for explanations of things I did not understand clearly. She also screened and scheduled visitors appropriately. She served as the focal point for communication regarding the state of my health, current diagnosis, and treatment. The list could go on, but I'm sure you can see the importance and difficulty of the role your primary support person is or could be playing.

Communication is certainly one of the key elements of the primary support person's role. I found it helpful to have Jana in the room each day when my doctors came by. My anxieties were such that I would not always hear the full explanation of some issue. She seemed to be a more effective listener under the circumstances, and I suspect this is often the case. Anyway, the two of us talked a lot about what the doctor had said, and she was often able to clarify things that I had missed. She could go ask nurses and others for additional explanations. In addition, she kept family, friends, and business associates informed about my progress. I did not find it productive for me to repeat time after time how sick I felt and the grim diagnosis I had been served by my physicians. Of course, the news wasn't always bad, but when it was, I sure didn't feel I benefited from dwelling on it.

It wasn't always easy for me to accept my wife's help. I felt I was a self-made man, and I was not accustomed to asking anyone for help. In fact, I felt that asking for help was a sign of weakness and failure. Eventually my health deteriorated to the point that I had no choice. I just couldn't provide for my needs without help from others. It certainly made things easier for everyone when I finally began asking for what I needed, from Jana and from all the others who offered their support.

Comments on Letters Thirteen, Fourteen, and Fifteen

One of the most difficult challenges in my life came during my father's struggle with serious illness, when I was thrust into looking at my work from the perspective of a family member and support person. I want to tell you about that experience. You may find it helpful to share these comments with members of your support team and point out how you feel and think about the subjects that come up.

When I went off to medical school, Dad was very pleased with my choice of profession. However, when I began to talk about the influence of the mind on healing, Dad, who was a Baptist minister, along with the rest of the family, felt that I was looking into pagan practices and the occult, and that my work was a culmination of those influences. They strongly preferred not to discuss any of it.

I had completed my residency and I had been assigned to Travis Air Force Base in California, where I was to be Chief of Radiation Therapy. Just as I arrived, the officer at the gate relayed an emergency call from my mother. My father was very ill. I took emergency leave before ever checking in and immediately went home.

It was after midnight when I arrived in Hollis, Oklahoma, a small town of just a few thousand people. I got to my father's hospital room just in time to see him lose consciousness. There was no doctor on duty, and I had to take the appropriate medical measures, shifting quickly from the role of son to physician.

The diagnosis was encephalitis, an infection of the brain. We had to transfer him the next morning to the University of Oklahoma Medical School Hospital in Oklahoma City. I rode with him during the harrowing 180-mile trip. The makeshift ambulance was really nothing more than a converted stationwagon. Still in a coma, my father became violent and violently ill during the trip. He was thrashing and pulling out his tubes. I saw that he could easily overpower me. As I struggled to restrain him, we both became covered with his vomit and diarrhea. I prayed for something to do, and I got an answer—sing. Sing lullabies, sing religious songs, sing anything. So as I laid there with my head on my father's chest, I sang and I cried. We both calmed down.

When we finally got to the hospital, I discovered the emergency room was no longer in service. My father's physician was away at a lecture. After much arguing, the nurse finally helped me find a room for him. I tried to get a physician to help me, but the few who were available did not wish to become involved with another doctor's patient. It was a very trying experience that left me feeling angry, confused, and physically ill.

Later that day, we were told that Dad was dying. I refused to accept that. Although this was only the fall of 1971, I was already very much involved in my work. The neurologist told us that if Dad did live, he would be "a vegetable." Dad's fever stayed up for days, peaking at 108 degrees. It took intense work to get it down.

During this time, I got tired of watching him fight, and I started wishing he would die. This made me very embarrassed and ashamed. I later came to appreciate how many people go through this with a loved one, this wanting them to die, wanting the struggle to be over.

Dad had a tube in his windpipe, he was on an artificial

respirator, and he had been completely comatose for nine days when a significant event occurred.

The family had gathered in Dad's room to watch the Texas–Oklahoma football game. Dad was an avid Oklahoma fan, and the "Sooners" won, soundly defeating Texas. At the end of the game, Dad spoke his first words. We credited the Sooners with contributing strongly to his coming out of the coma.

Dad recovered slowly. He had profound neurological deficits, but he overcame all of those, only to experience heart difficulties. While he was in coronary intensive care, one of the staff physicians mentioned to him that people could consciously influence their heart rate. Dad was on a monitor and he started experimenting with different thoughts. He found that he could shift his heart rate dramatically by shifting what he was thinking. He got very excited and called the staff person in and told him that his son had been talking about these concepts for some time. He was quite shocked when the house staffer didn't want to know any more about me.

As soon as Dad got out of the hospital, he called and told me about the entire episode. Then he asked if I could come out and help him understand more about how to use his mind to get better. I was on the first flight I could arrange.

Together, he and I planned a meditative course, and I made him a meditation tape to regain his health. He had a profound response, dramatically controlling his high blood pressure and coming off anti-hypertensive medicine.

He did very well for several years, until he had a heart attack. Once again, he asked me to help him get well, and I agreed. He left the hospital in short order, regaining his health very dramatically. Within the calendar year, he competed in the Seniors of the National Rodeo Timed Events, at sixty-eight years old.

He and my mother went through one of my early patient sessions, which was a very exciting but challenging experience for me. I helped him deal with his high blood pressure, his heart disease, and his heart attack. I taught him the basics of the mind/body relationship, and he became more interested in this work than I had ever imagined he would be.

After he retired from the ministry, he worked at a nursing home where he started teaching meditation. He said that meditation always put him in the proper state of mind for prayer, and he used prayer and meditation together. He also said meditation was more powerful than any medication he ever took.

Dad actually worked with a couple of patients who were sent to his nursing home with terminal cancer but got well enough to go home again. He also had plenty of patients for me to see. Every time I went home for a visit, he had a group of people lined up in the living room.

From all these experiences, I knew that Dad had a strong belief in my work and a great ability to heal himself. But then he was diagnosed with cancer.

Prior to the diagnosis of cancer, one of Dad's grandsons, my nephew, had committed suicide. While the entire family grieved, I saw my Dad quit living as a response to that suicide. He blamed himself for it, as well as for many, many other circumstances in his life that were beyond his control. It was sad, but he reached a point where there was just too much anguish in his life for him to want to go on.

Even when he called and told me to come and help him, his voice told me he didn't really want me to help him get well. I went home anyway, of course. I knew he could do the work if he wanted to, but it was soon very clear that he would not make even the smallest effort.

We had a family meeting to decide upon an approach. We thought that the best position to take was that we wanted Dad to get well, but that it was okay for him to die. We would support him in his decision, no matter what it was. This was agreed to by everyone except Mother. Mother said no, she would not support his dying. They had been married since she was sixteen, and even if he was struggling, he at least was alive. She said she would rather have him alive and suffering than dead. It was a very honest response, so acknowledging her wishes as the primary support person, we proceeded to try to get Dad to live.

Dad didn't cooperate. One of the activities in the program he and I planned was that he was to get dressed once a day, four days a week. He had been doing this previously, but after the first three days of the program, he hadn't dressed once. The idea had been to reward him for something he was already doing. It didn't work out that way. We decided, in another family meeting, to confront him with this and also with the fact that he was being very harsh with my eldest sister, whose job it was to ask him each day about what he was doing. The confrontation was very sorrowful and touching. We ended up talking about the need to be kinder to one another and about the fact that we were all fighting for the same thing.

Dad said that he was going to push ahead, muster his forces and really try to get well. However, a few days later, after I had gone home, he told my mother he couldn't do it, he was throwing in the towel. We had never heard him use that term before, even though he had been a boxer in his early years.

I flew back to see him as soon as I heard. Here was the person I loved the most, knew the most about, had the most experience working with, and I could see that I was powerless to do anything more than love him. He couldn't say he wanted to die, and I don't think he wanted to die, he just wanted out of the pain of life. He was seventy, and he believed he had lived long enough.

I told him that I loved him and we exchanged other tender messages. He told me he didn't want to live on for a long time. I said that it made sense to me that he would not want to linger on in his condition and that I could understand his wanting to be with the ones he loved on the other side. He said he wished he could get some help; he wished he could work at dying as he had worked at living. I told him he could, that he could use the same techniques he had used to get well to help him let go of life. He became very still and curious, and he asked me to explain.

I told him he could simply meditate about turning loose of life and going to be with God. As I said that, he lay back into the bed. I could see his face become very peaceful. We kissed each other good-bye. That was the last time I saw him. He died five days after that conversation, very quietly.

My father had lived when he wanted to live, and he died when he was ready to die. To me, that's what success with this work is all about. It is helping people to get well when they want to get well, and helping them to die when they want to die. It's loving them and supporting them while they are confused and don't know if they want to live or die. This work is about loving people; it's about loving yourself.

My father was my favorite patient. I loved him more than I've loved any other person I've had a chance to work with. I knew him better than I've ever known anyone else. From him, I gained first-hand knowledge of what it's like to have a family member diagnosed with a serious illness, and I had the opportunity to grow both through his decision to live and through his unspoken decision to die.

The experience of illness is bound to bring forth a family's strengths as well as its weaknesses. Because my father was a minister and my brother-in-law and I were doctors, we had open lines of communication about subjects that other families may find difficult to discuss. We could talk about our spiritual beliefs. We could talk about illness and treatment. We could talk about living and dying.

It is most important that your family have open communication at this time. Family members who find it difficult to take part in the support system may want to get counseling, but don't force them to do so. Each family member has to deal with the situation in his or her own way and time. These family members also need your understanding and patience. Be assured that each will do the best he or she can, given who each is.

I believe that the more open a person is to experiencing the life and death of another, the more open they are to their own life experience and the less afraid they are of their own death.

I have learned that if I become attached to a person's getting well, if I think he or she has to get well, then I am in an unhealthy place. I am also being an unhealthy influence. I have given that person a goal, an absolute, rather than an aim or direction. I have imprisoned them. They have to get well or will have failed, according to the goal I have set for them.

It is very important that the support person not do this to the person with a life-threatening illness. You can say, "I want you to get well. I want you in my life. I want you to be healthy, happy, and fulfilled. I want us to grow old together. I want us to realize the things we have always wanted." But it is important not to become attached to the outcome.

You burden the sick person when you attach yourself to the outcome of his or her efforts to get well. You need to add, at least to your own thinking, another agreement: "It's okay with me if you die. It's not what I want, but that's okay." This doesn't have to be communicated verbally—in fact, it may be quite inappropriate to do so. It is an internal message communicated in your attitude. It puts the sick person in a win/win situation. They win if they live, they don't fail if they die. This is sometimes very difficult work for members of a support team, but it is very important.

The last point I want to make is perhaps the most important: You cannot get well for the sick person. You can only support his or her efforts to get well. Let the sick person decide what you can do to be supportive. Be honest about whether or not you can take on the challenge of your role. Keep your primary focus on your own health and well-being while being sensitive to the ill person's needs so that you have the energy to be supportive over the course of the disease.

If you are facing illness in the family right now, plan a family meeting to discuss the roles of each family member and how these roles will be played out. Family and support team members may or may not find it comfortable to hold these discussions with the patient present. In any case, make sure that the patient knows about the meeting and is consulted about what role he or she would like each person to play. Then give the patient feedback on what resulted so that he or she can adjust expectations accordingly.

Another practical strategy for any member of the support team is to schedule a session with a therapist to discuss your feelings and experience. You may see the same therapist the patient uses or a different one, but do this with the intent of taking care of your own needs, not the patient's. Your patient may not be as considerate as Reid was. He or she may not be able to respect your needs because his or her own seem so overwhelming at this time. It is your responsibility to let the patient know you have needs and that one of them is to feel free to take time off from your support role to take care of yourself. Relay this message with conscious consideration and forethought, if possible at a time when you both are calm, rather than under the stress of a crisis. But be sure to ask for what you want.

——————— SIXTEEN

The Role of the Physician

Dear Friend,

I have a lot of reservations about what is going on with the health care system in this country. However, it is the one I had to deal with when I was sick. I decided I could make better choices as an informed patient. This is some of what I learned about physicians and their role within the system.

To begin with, many physicians invest up to fourteen years of their lives to obtain the training required to practice medicine in this country. The average medical doctor will graduate at roughly twenty-nine years of age to begin practice. Often significant debts are incurred for education—many doctors have heavy debts from borrowing to pay their way through medical school—moving to a location where a practice can be established, and setting up a practice. Malpractice insurance costs vary but can run to tens of thousands of dollars a year for certain specialties. Add to this the costs of running an office (rent, salaries for support personnel, and administrative costs).

Most medical students undergo rigorous training in many different areas. The methodology employed is highly quantitative and scientific in nature, with technology playing an increasingly visible role. The rate of change is so rapid that a physician can quickly fall behind in new developments unless he or she spends lots of time studying, and many do. It is very easy for a doctor to become "technologically obsolete" these days, which places additional stress and strain on a person who already conducts his or her role under a lot of pressure.

More than one doctor has gone through medical school with the expectation or hope of developing a cure for some major disease. Some, of course, do make major contributions of this type. Many more, however, go into practice and find it a rather hum-drum existence: The hours are long and often filled with legal and administrative headaches. The work is not as interesting as might be expected—most patients have rather mundane problems that are treated in a largely routine fashion. In fact, some physicians estimate that approximately 70 percent of all the patients they see neither need nor benefit from their services. Patients who do need help often blame their doctor when the doctor is unable to fix them after they themselves have neglected their health for long periods of time. In addition, patients often just won't cooperate with their physicians or take part in their own recovery process.

In view of the foregoing, it is not surprising to learn that many doctors find their practices unfulfilling. Even under the best of working conditions, doctors often have difficult family lives due to the long hours, telephone interruptions, untimely hospital visits, deaths of patients, and the related stress of balancing all of this with the needs of a spouse and children.

I knew I couldn't solve the problems of all the physicians in our health care system, but I could do something. I could play my role as a patient with understanding and compassion, and I could take responsibility for contributing to my healing process in whatever ways were appropriate and necessary for my survival. I could also act to insure that all who were involved in my treatment knew that I sincerely wanted and appreciated their efforts.

_____ SEVENTEEN

The Doctor–Patient Relationship

Dear Friend,

I believe it was helpful to select a doctor with appropriate skills and an outlook somewhat in harmony with mine, especially with regard to the connection between body, mind, and spirit. However, once chosen, I think it was as important for me to respect my doctor's view as it was for the doctor to respect mine.

I did not feel compelled to tell my doctor how to do his or her job. I could and did listen respectfully, understanding that the doctor was doing his or her best to give me some valuable input regarding his or her current view of my physical processes.

Here are some specific examples of how I attempted to contribute to good relationships with my doctors:

• Although I felt free to ask my doctors for any needed information, I did not knowingly waste their time with questions a nurse or administrative person could answer.

• I was considerate of my doctors' feelings, encouraging them to do their best under the circumstances. I explained that I had faith in God and that I was ready to go when God took me and that I would appreciate each doctor's efforts no matter what happened. I made it clear that I was no longer infatuated with blaming others. I hoped this would take any undue pressure off the doctor to back up his or her work with unnecessary tests, which were sometimes painful or uncomfortable.

• I made it clear that I was open to alternative methods, drugs, therapies, etc. I also made it clear that I wanted to take part in the decision-making process when options were available. Some of my physicians seemed to genuinely appreciate my willingness to help in choosing the course of treatment.

• I showed an interest in my doctors as people. I learned about their families, interests, hobbies, and so forth whenever possible.

• I sent my doctors modest gifts and thank-you notes to let them know I really did appreciate their efforts on my behalf.

• I made it a point to let my doctors know that I was really trying to help myself get well. We had the same objective. They knew I was cooperative and dedicated, and I believe my attitudes and efforts stimulated their best work on my behalf.

I chose to see doctors as trained people who have a lot of scientific, technical, and practical medical expertise and experience—they are valuable resources to be called on for assistance in dealing with the human body. They did not make me sick and, in and of themselves, I did not believe they could make me well. They could, I thought, be one of several channels through which healing would be sent from God to me. They could also provide additional comfort while the process was unfolding.

Although I greatly appreciated the contributions of medicine in my recovery, I did not rely solely on doctors, nor did I see them as the final authority on my health. After all, they were dealing with the physical aspect of "Reid," while I made efforts also to take care of the mental and spiritual aspects of "Reid." I deeply believed that my spiritual and mental aspects could make a crucial difference in my healing.

I found it helpful to think of the doctor as being like a football coach on the sidelines. He can call the plays (medicines, treatment, guidance, etc.), but he does not personally participate in the game of life taking place between God and me. This doctor/coach analogy helped to reinforce the importance of my role as a participating patient and God's role as the source of healing.

I believe that doctors facilitate the healing process in the human body and that this service can provide the time, comfort, and energy needed to make the physical, mental, and spiritual changes necessary for a healthy life. This does not mean that doctors are infallible or that the medical system in this country is without problems.

Before my experience with cancer, I was rather naive about medicine. I simply had not been sick much in the first forty years of my life. I thought the health care system in this country was highly ingenious and could do just about anything. However, this is the deal I was offered by traditional medicine: "We don't know the cause of hairy cell leukemia, we have no effective treatment for it, and we are not and will not be working on one. You will probably die within a few years, spend tens of thousands of dollars on treatment, undergo countless painful procedures, be uncomfortable much of the time, and there is no alternative that we know about."

This was a rude awakening, but also a blessing in disguise. It brought me to the realization that I would have to play a key role in regaining my health. This is not to say that I didn't benefit from medicine. I did. I have taken many helpful drugs, had countless transfusions, operations, etc. I believe in medicine. I also believe that spirit, mind, and body operate in tandem in getting sick or getting well. My doctors' primary role was to take care of my physical body. The rest was up to me, my support persons (including psychologists), and my Creator.

Slowly I came to believe that the wisdom that operates the human body knows exactly what it's doing. The body is a highly organized and interdependent system. In the case of certain health problems, it may take a long time for changes to emerge in my body, whether I feel those changes should happen slowly or not. I learned that blood cells live about 120 days. In my case, months sometimes elapsed before the changes occurring in my body (resulting from mental-spiritual changes) manifested on a level that doctors could measure or that I could feel.

I created a practical plan. I decided that while my doctors were working on my body, I would work on my mind and spirit. Maybe all three—body, mind, and spirit— would improve together. I believe that is what happened.

_____ *EIGHTEEN*

Becoming Your Own Health Manager

Dear Friend,

Although I didn't think of it in this way initially, I now see that it would have been helpful if I had seen myself as my own "health manager" from the outset of my cancer experience. Over the years I began to look at my problem from my perspective as the manager of a business. I saw myself organizing the resources at my disposal to work on the problem (my health) in the most effective way possible.

I became the manager of all the resources involved in my cancer experience, and I accepted full responsibility for the results. I believed that all the choices were ultimately mine, including all those that had preceded the diagnosis.

I decided I would see myself as having hired a variety of specialists to provide needed services for my body. Those specialists included doctors, nurses, x-ray technicians, lab technicians, hospital staff, clinic staff, nutritionists, physical therapists, masseurs, and others.

For help with my mental processes, I hired psychologists and psychiatrists. For a long time after my leukemia was diagnosed, it did not occur to me to seek the counsel of a psychologist. Eventually, I did and, as I have discussed, it was very productive. He presented different points of view, ideas, and questions that I might never have thought of on my own, or at least would not have uncovered as quickly by myself. He served as a stimulus and a guide, encouraging me to work on difficult and painful personal issues I had been ignoring. He proved to be a non-threatening, impartial, and experienced resource that was of great value to me.

I also called on the pastor of the church I attended for spiritual guidance and prayer support, and I began to rely more heavily on my immediate support group, including my wife, family, close friends, and business associates. Initially in my cancer experience, I didn't tell my parents I was sick because I didn't want to burden them. Besides, I didn't feel there was anything they could do for me. Later, after I told my mother about my illness and my reasons for not telling her sooner, she told me that she could have helped me from the outset through prayer. I now agree whole-heartedly! One of my brothers proved to be a potentially valuable resource. His white blood cells proved to be almost identical to mine, which meant a white cell transfusion was possible. Even though this was never done, it was comforting to know it was feasible and that he was willing.

I used my organizational skills to manage my health care system in much the same way I had managed my family support system. Notice that I use the word "support." This reflects my belief that we, as patients, play a pivotal role in our own recovery. Thus, I feel it is most productive to see others as supporting or assisting us in accomplishing the purposes we have chosen.

I realized that each person in my health care team would offer services in accord with his or her specialty, training, experience, and beliefs. I also was willing for each person to offer these services in his or her own unique way. However, if I found someone's uniqueness getting in the way of sensible treatment, I replaced him or her with someone who worked better for me. I do not encourage you to make emotionally inspired changes of doctors and hospitals, but I do feel that considering alternatives and getting second opinions can be helpful. I found that training, experience, and skill levels vary considerably from doctor to doctor. Some hospitals employ more advanced treatment in certain specialties than others. All are not equal. Larger is not necessarily better. At any rate, I decided to exercise my power to choose who and what would be part of my health care system. But I did not do this until I had a clear understanding of the situation and had examined alternatives with input from the appropriate parties.

I found that just as some family members are not in a position to help when serious illness occurs, the same is true of some doctors. Their inability to contribute may reflect their training, personality, limited experience, depleted physical stamina, frayed nerves, or whatever. In any case, I realized that I was not going to reshape either family members or doctors during serious bouts of illness. I could, however, choose to manage my health resources in a productive way to benefit my health.

I hope you don't get the idea that I was a difficult patient. Instead, I realized that the members of my health care support team did not make me sick and were trying to help with my recovery. Although I would sometimes become frustrated, I realized that people are not often inspired to do their best work by unappreciative patients. I tried to conduct myself in a way that would elicit the most helpful response under the circumstances. I found it much to my advantage to be a cooperative patient if I was to expect the best from those being asked for help.

I also realized that I could not change the medical system and shouldn't try to do so while I was experiencing a life-threatening illness. I could, however, change my interaction with the health care system and use it to my benefit, concentrating on a balanced effort—physical, mental, and spiritual—to move toward health.

Comments on Letters Sixteen, Seventeen, and Eighteen

In dealing with patients, I find I have the most success with those who believe in my ability to help them, and who are also confident and enthusiastic about their treatment and their ability to get well again. Of the patients who come to the Simonton Cancer Center, most are willing to take that extra step to beat their disease. Some, however, are simply desperate for any help, their beliefs tenuous, at best. Others, who have been persuaded to come, are looking for flaws in our approach, to justify their belief: "I knew this wouldn't work." In most cases, this is an acquired belief, for, like Reid, these patients have been assured by more than one medical authority that they cannot be helped. At the Simonton Cancer Center we are accustomed to being challenged by our patients, and we are comfortable working with people who are filled with doubt.

Many fine physicians do have a profound understanding and appreciation for their patients' healing powers. Keep in mind that your doctor is trained in the prevailing beliefs of the medical profession. He or she may be an excellent technician, but that doesn't make him or her a skilled healer. It is my belief that many physicians approached their profession as natural healers and, having had that trained out of them in medical school, must rekindle their natural ability. If you can learn to view your doctor's negative attitude as just one person's beliefs, rather than being overwhelmed by his or her authority and accepting these beliefs as truth, you can be much more objective in your evaluation of the care you are receiving. This is especially important when your physician seems to have no regard for your attitude toward healing and projects a belief that you have no chance of getting well.

In traditional Chinese medicine, the doctor was fired if the patient got sick. I like that system. It gave the doctor a vested interest—one that we don't always see today—in keeping the patient healthy. Although interest in preventive medicine is increasing in this country, the emphasis is still on treating sick people rather than on preventing their illness in the first place.

It has been reported in the *Annals of the New York Academy of Science* that healing works best when the patient believes in the healer and when the healer believes in his or her own methods. Evaluate your relationship with your doctor in these terms. What do you believe to be true about your doctor? What indications do you have that your doctor believes in his or her methods of treatment?

Another way to evaluate your relationship with your doctor is to consider how well you communicate with one another. As Reid points out, medical conversation often becomes clouded by emotions, particularly fear, and also by the technical jargon used to describe procedures and treatments. To gain some insight into your present level of communication, make a list of your beliefs about your doctor and about your treatment as you understand it. Evaluate how healthy these beliefs are. Keep the healthy beliefs, and change the unhealthy ones, using the techniques you have already learned. This will produce healthy emotions that, in turn, will move your body's healing system in the direction of health. When you are meditating, simply ask your inner wisdom what information would help to increase your trust in your doctor and your treatment. Be sure to balance this with work on trusting your own body and its processes.

By now the answer to the question "Who is responsible for the physical care of your body, you or the doctor?" should be abundantly clear. The answer, of course, is both. Your doctor is responsible for determining the diagnosis and for the way it is presented to you. This responsibility includes advising you about treatment options and making the best ones available to you.

You are responsible for deciding on treatment and cooperating with the treatment and with your health care team. You are also responsible for your beliefs and the resultant emotions, which will have an important effect on how you respond to your diagnosis and treatment.

It has been my experience that patients benefit most from what they learn from themselves, rather than just from reading or hearing information from other sources (although that, too, is important). I know, at my deepest levels of consciousness, that within each of us is the inner wisdom that is the source of all healing. We try to lead patients toward experiences of this inner wisdom during the week they are with us at the Simonton Cancer Center. We believe they will take these experiences home, together with all the other tools they acquire, and begin to build trust in their own healing abilities. I hope this book can help you do the same.

I believe that a skilled healer—whether a physician, counselor, minister, shaman, medicine man, or simply a friend or relative, or any combination of these—is one who helps you stretch your imagination in the direction of hope, harmony, and health. When you are around such a person, you feel good, comfortable, safe, and protected. When you are with a person who triggers your imagination in unhealthy directions, you feel bad—confused, hopeless, depressed, or fearful.

If you believe you cannot cope with the pain of a

particular treatment, be open about it. Tell your doctor. It doesn't help matters to suffer in silence. He or she may be able to offer an alternative treatment. Make the best choice available. Know that you have done the very best you can for your body. Often a therapist can help you by exploring your beliefs about the treatment, and through imagery exercises geared toward cooperating with your particular treatment. You may also want to talk with other cancer patients who have used the treatment successfully. What enabled them to cope? Remember always that your inner wisdom knows the best way for you to get well. Use this resource regularly.

When you are undergoing any medical treatment, honor the process, respect its effects. Chemotherapy and radiation can reduce your energy, so take time to rest. Delegate the tasks of life. Ask for whatever help you need. In fact, use periods of treatment as opportunities for learning to ask for what you want at other times as well.

As you continue to become better acquainted with your body and become more adept at influencing it in positive ways, you can gradually assume more responsibility for your healing. When you feel this happening, introduce yourself to the new health manager in your life. Yourself.

_____ *NINETEEN*

Responding to Recurrence

Dear Friend,

I felt wonderful for quite a while after the miraculous recovery I experienced in the fall of 1981. I was stronger than ever and had a marvelous spiritual life that was full of joy. I had enjoyed periods of happiness before in my life, but never anything like the joy I experienced during these years. I felt very close to God and was surrounded by a sense of peace and well-being.

I began to have a deep desire to share my miraculous recovery with others. In due course, it seemed desirable to write a series of letters explaining my experience. I began doing this in 1982. But after a limited number of letters, I no longer seemed to have the flow of information to share.

I eventually understood why my writings were terminated. For some reason, I had begun to believe that I had discovered some combination of ingredients that *caused* this miracle to occur. After all, I had spent untold hours studying hypnosis, meditation, diet, exercise, food supplements, physiology, psychology, philosophy, religion, and many other subjects. I felt certain that some specific mental process triggered spiritual healing and that I had found it, although I was unsure of the exact combination of things I had done.

Note that I emphasized what *I* had done to cause this miracle. In retrospect, it seems absolutely ridiculous that anyone would come to such a conclusion. I now believe the flow of information for the letters halted because the understanding I would have communicated was unhealthy. I didn't realize this at the time. I simply thought I could no longer write "meaningfully," that I just didn't have anything else to say.

As my writing came to a halt, I had the distinct understanding that I had not learned some of my "cancer lessons." Somehow I knew I was going to have cancer again. I knew the reason was to enable me to learn what I had failed to learn before.

Some time later, I could feel things happening in my body. Eventually, I went to my doctor who confirmed that my leukemia had returned.

Please understand that I am definitely not implying that everyone needs cancer to learn life's lessons. However, in my case, I needed something to awaken me, and cancer did that once again.

For this second cancer experience, my attitude was rather matter-of-fact because I saw this episode as a learning process. My spiritual aspect had told me this was the case beforehand. The recurrence was not unexpected. I didn't know what I needed to learn, but I knew learning was the purpose of this cancer episode, as it was of the one that preceded it.

I do not mean to imply that I had no fear. Since I had been miraculously healed once before, I knew God was on my side, although I didn't know why. I really believed I would get well again, but I did not know how or when. Consequently, most of my fear was related to the pain and discomfort associated with the hospital visits and treatments. I certainly wrestled with doubts about my eventual health. In fact, I had plenty of doubts about my abilities as I so obviously had failed to learn what I needed to know from my first cancer experience. I was afraid God would get tired of wasting his time on a slow learner.

I was very sick during this period. I went to a different hospital this time where the nurses, who were specialists in working with cancer patients, commented that they had never seen anyone with blood counts as low as mine. Some came from other floors just to see what I looked like. Jana later told me that they were amazed at my positive attitude. They seemed even more surprised when I got out of bed and walked up and down the hall for exercise. Of course, I didn't walk very fast or very far. But even sitting up in bed was most unexpected under the circumstances.

I contracted all sorts of infections, sometimes two or three at a time. I received an array of powerful drugs intravenously. The infections would clear up, my doctors would stop the drugs, and I would get the same infections again or even more difficult ones.

Then one day I had another spiritual experience. I had been studying for many days what the Bible says about faith, and my faith had indeed been strengthened as a result. In a rather dreamlike state, I was told that I would be well by the beginning of December. This happened in early November, as I recall. I understood this message to mean that my body would begin producing proper blood cells on December first. This meant that I would begin feeling better soon thereafter and would have normal blood counts sometime in April. (As I have pointed out before, red blood cells live roughly 120 days.) That's exactly what unfolded. My blood counts were basically in the normal range around the beginning of April.

During this entire episode of cancer, I was on a "miracle drug." I almost died while taking it. I also got well while taking the same drug. But note that my health returned exactly in accordance with the spiritual message I received. I presume the drugs and related treatments were indeed helpful in various ways. However, insofar as I am concerned, my healing was precipitated in a spiritual way. When you evaluate this, please consider that I alone lived this experience—the recurrence, the message, and the return to health—and I am describing it the best way I know how.

This second cancer episode had indeed been an important learning experience for me. I started this letter by telling you that I had focused on what I had done to get well. *I should have focused on what God had done for me.* I now envision my mind as being like a mold (or matrix) containing beliefs that can enhance, block, or distort the flow of the creative force generated by God and sent to all of us. I came to realize that I could best serve if I focused on what God can do through me rather than on what I can do through God. Once again, I see the response I chose as being more powerful than the problem itself.

Comments on Letter Nineteen

In my opinion, the best way to deal with recurrence is not to make it more important than it is. While every patient wants to find a treatment—traditional or otherwise—that works immediately and permanently, this is not always the case. Recovery from anything requires a continual evaluation of what is going on, and that often includes times when things are not going as well as one would hope. That does not mean that recovery is not possible: It means that there will likely be some ups and downs along the way. Finding the reserves to deal with these ups and downs is one of the most difficult aspects of getting well, and support is vital in this area.

Please do not take the diagnosis of recurrence as a death sentence. Try to allow yourself some time to absorb the shock. Then, as you have done before, use meditation to ask what the message of the recurrence is and act on that message. Acknowledge that you have done the best you could with the information you had at the time.

Recurrence is a possibility for any cancer patient. It is a subject that you should feel free to discuss rather than ignore, and once again, if you can't discuss your fears around it now, get some help from a professional who can hear you out and guide you. Be assured that discussing your fear of recurrence does not result in recurrence. It does help to relieve you of negative emotions by developing healthier beliefs about recurrence. This can lessen the importance of recurrence whether it happens or not.

If you do experience a recurrence, look at it just as you have been looking at your health all along. Use it for

feedback. You may have unresolved conflicts that have re-
surfaced and need resolving. You may still be getting your
needs met through illness, not having found any other way
to take care of them. You may be overwhelmed by all the
changes you have made and need to slow down. You may
have stopped doing some of the things that were having a
positive impact on your health. Ask about these things in
meditation. Reevaluate your two-year health plan. Do you
need to put more emphasis on doing the work outlined, or
do you now need to make some changes in your plan?

This is also a time to reinforce your support system and
rely on it more than you have in the past. Let others help
you as much as is reasonable so that you can concentrate on
taking care of yourself.

With his recurrence, Reid took another look at his
definition of cancer to try to explain why it had again manifested. Having framed cancer within a healthy and positive
definition of life during his first experience, he felt less fear
when it occurred again.

Reid defined cancer as blocked spiritual flows. That
definition may not be helpful to you; but for Reid, it
continued to provide insight into what he could do about
his illness. He needed to remove those blocks that prevented spirit from acting on his life.

My own translation of Reid's concept is to speak of a
block in our understanding of our relationship to ourselves,
to the planet, or to all there is. Certain beliefs can interfere
with that relationship, while other beliefs can foster a
strong, harmonious relationship.

We can also relate Reid's concept to the definition of
cancer that I offered earlier. A part of the experience of cancer
is trying to be who you are not, which could be explained as
being out of the natural flow of the universe or being
blocked from the flow of energy that keeps the universe in

motion. *Healing from cancer involves becoming who you are,* which means removing the blocks and becoming part of the flow of the universe, becoming more in harmony with your true nature.

I think Reid's definition is similar to my own, the same thing said two different ways. This doesn't mean that we are "right"; it just means that we share similar beliefs.

If you are experiencing a recurrence, give some thought to your own definition of cancer. What does it indicate about your beliefs? How does it enable you to act on your cancer? If your definition of cancer is not healthy or helpful to you, work with Reid's definition—or with mine—to develop a new definition of your own.

In meditation, explore what you consider to be the main obstacle to your healing and ask your inner wisdom how to use that obstacle as an opportunity for learning.

If you are responding to recurrence with feelings of failure, guilt, or blame, remember to practice the belief: "I always do the best I can with the information and understanding I have at the time." Be gentle with yourself and get help. I find that people I work with seldom experience feelings of guilt, failure, or blame longer than a few days. Remember we create those feelings with our beliefs and attitudes, so the work is to change the unhealthy beliefs to healthier beliefs.

_____ TWENTY

What I Have Learned

Dear Friend,

As you will recall, my thoughts about God and his creation were confusing and disorganized at the beginning of my cancer experience in 1979. Things have changed. I now have some rather definite points of view. I hope this summary will prove useful. Summarizing your own thoughts in a similar way—and reviewing and updating them occasionally—is likely to be helpful to you, as well.

- God's creation exists to serve his purposes, not mine.
- I am part of God's creation; he is not part of mine.
- God's creation is alive, interactive, interdependent, ongoing.
- I am not presently aware of all of God's creation.
- Each aspect of God's creation has a particular role or function that is necessary and related in some way to the operation of the entire universe.
- God's creation is always moving toward spiritual balance. Each action initiates a reaction; a movement away from balance initiates a counter-movement toward balance.
- There is no such thing as an isolated stimulus. Every

thought, word, or action by any aspect of creation initiates a reaction. However, we may not be aware of such realities as they occur.

• There is no such thing as "independence" from God. We cannot detach ourselves from God's creation. My belief in "independence" was an error based on my misunderstanding of God.

• It is not possible for me to alter God's grand design for his creation in any way. His purposes will be accomplished irrespective of my choices. It is, however, possible for me to express myself creatively in many ways within my role in God's creation.

• The highest life experience is created when I choose to express myself by pursuing a life purpose that is in harmony with God's creation. If I choose a purpose that is not in harmony with God's creation, I will not be in harmony with the deepest levels of myself.

• My choices have a dramatic bearing on the creation of my own personal perception of reality.

• We humans have a tendency to focus on our own creations rather than on God's. We are given what we need, but our understanding of our needs is limited by our own concepts. Many of us therefore unwittingly choose to use only a minute portion of the potential power available to us. We stay within the very limited sphere of a self-serving entity, rather than choosing to serve the totality of creation.

• We can choose to see ourselves as an integral part of the whole creation, and to realize that the creation of which we are part is in itself infinite.

• An individualistic, self-serving point of view is necessarily limiting, and as such, attracts only a limited supply of creative energy.

• We can choose to see ourselves as serving God's creation rather than being served by it. We thereby transcend our focus on ourselves and come to play a role that is *in* this dimension but not *of* this dimension.

• As we become more and more aware of our true spiritual nature, we also become less and less infatuated with the mind and the physical body. The perception of separation between spirit and body may help us to understand death from this physical dimension. This view tends to minimize the fear of death.

• Every aspect of God's creation is alive and designed to teach us what we need to know in order to become what God wants us to be. This includes being loving, kind, caring, compassionate, understanding, obedient to God, harmonious with God's creations, and joyful.

• We experience harmony when we choose in a manner consistent with God's creation. This is an enjoyable process, and the body adapts accordingly.

• In making choices, we interact with life, the teacher, and produce meaningful, specific results from which we always have the opportunity to learn and grow. As students of God, we come to realize that some responses are more productive than others.

• Sometimes we become frustrated with life and see learning about God as hopeless. This can affect our will to live or our desire to continue to interact with life. But we can choose again, and choose differently.

• As a guest on this planet, a student of life, and a willing servant, I can choose a more enlightened path and experience physical transformation, joy, and harmony in this dimension by realizing and accepting God's love in the here and now.

In closing, I feel compelled to remind you that I am sharing what I believe only to serve you, to stimulate your thoughts. It is my deepest prayer that you will be able to benefit from these thoughts and experiences as you reconsider how God affects your life.

Concluding Comments

I hope that this final letter has given you further insight into your beliefs and that all of Reid's letters have been a powerful stimulant and guide as you move toward health.

At this point, if you have worked through the book, you have completed your two-year health plan and have made meditation and imagery part of your daily practice. Hopefully, you have also recognized some experiences of your inner wisdom and have gained confidence in your body's ability to heal itself.

But the work is not over. The work in this book is part of the life-long process of becoming who you are. Compare your emotions, thoughts, and beliefs about cancer to what they were when you began this work. Does your attitude toward your health reflect healthy changes in your beliefs?

As you continue on your healing journey, you can use this book over and over again. Your creativity is the only limitation to your work. Review the list of letters, prioritize them according to your present needs, and work through the letter series again. Or write your own letters, based on your work in this book. Even if you don't send them to anyone, they'll be a wonderful way to continue observing your beliefs.

You can also take the skills you have learned in this book and use them to explore other approaches to healing.

I want you to know that Reid and I truly support your efforts. We hope that you will continue to grow in understanding, expanding your consciousness and opening your heart to discover whatever you need to know to enjoy good health and a fulfilling life.

Medical Bibliography
(Research Background for Chapter 1)

Ader, R., Cohen, N. (1982). Behaviorally conditioned immunosuppression and systemic lupis erythematosis. *Science*, 19, March. 215:1534–1536.

Ader, R., Cohen N. (1981). Conditioned immunopharmacologic effects. In: *Psychoneuroimmunology*. New York: Academic Press.

Ader, R., Felton D. (1990). *Psychoneuroimmunology II*. New York: Academic Press.

Berk, L. S., Tan, S. A., Napier, B. J., Eby, W. C. (1989). Eustress of mirthful laughter modifies natural killer cell activity. *Clinical Research*. National Meeting, Washington D.C. April 18–May 1.

Berk, L. S., Tan, S. A., Nehlsen-Cannarella, S., Napier, B. J., Lewis, J. E., Lee, J. W., Eby, W. C. (1988). Humor associated laughter decreases cortisol and increases spontaneous lymphocyte blastogenesis. *Clinical Research*. 36:435A.

Berk, L. S., Tan, S. A., Fry, W. F., Napier, B. J., Lee, J. W., Hubbard, R. W., Lewis, J. E., Eby, W. C. (1989). Neuroendocrine and stress hormone changes during mirthful laughter. *The American Journal of the Medical Sciences*. December. 296: No. 7:390–396.

Pulloch, K. (1985). Neuroanatomy of lymphoid tissue: a review in Guillemin Cohn, Melnechuk, (eds). *Neural Modulation of Immunity.* New York: Raven. pp. 111–140.

Derogatis, L., Abeloff, M., Melisaratos, N. (1979). Psychological coping mechanisms and survival time in metastatic breast cancer. *Journal of the American Medical Association.* 242:1504–1508.

Eysenck, H. J. (1988). Health's character. *Psychology Today.* December. Vol. 22, pp. 28–32.

Felton, D. L., Livnat, S., Carlson, S. L., Bellinger, D. L., Yeh, P. (1984). Sympathetic innervation of lymph nodes in mice. *Brain Research Bulletin.* December. 13:693–699.

Greer, S. and McEwan, P.J.M. (eds) 1985. Cancer and the Mind. *Soc. Sci. Med.,* 20:771–853.

Grossarth-Maticek, Ronald, Bastiaan Jan, and Kanazir Dusan. Psychosocial factors as strong predictions of mortality from cancer, ischemic heart disease and stroke: Yugoslav Prospective Study. 1985, *Journal of Psychosomatic Research.* Vol. 29, pp. 167–176.

Kiecolt-Glaser, J. K., Garner, W., Speicher, C. E., Penn, G., Glaser, R. (1984). Psychosocial modifiers of immunocompetence in medical students. *Psychosomatic Medicine.* 46:7–14.

Klopfer, B. (1957). Psychological variables in human cancer. *Journal of Projective Techniques.* 21:331–340.

LeShan, L. (1989). *Cancer As A Turning Point,* New York: E. P. Dutton.

New York Academy of Science. (1966). Psychophysiological aspects of cancer. Vol. 125.

New York Academy of Science (1969). Psychological aspects of cancer. Vol. 164.

Ornish, Dean. (1990) Can lifestyle changes reverse coronary heart disease? *Lancet.* July 21, 1990. 336(8708):129–133.

Pert, C. B. (1986). The wisdom of the receptors: neuropeptides, the emotions, and bodymind. *Advances* 3(3):8–16.

Pert, C. B., Ruff, M. R., Weber, R. J., Herkenham, M. (1985). Neuropeptides and their receptors: a psychosomatic network. *Journal of Immunology.* 135:820s–826s.

Simonton, O. C., Matthews-Simonton, S. S. (1975). Belief systems and management of the emotional aspects of malignancy. *Journal of Transpersonal Psychology.* 7(1):29–47.

Simonton, O. C., Matthews-Simonton, S., Creighton, J. L. (1978). *Getting Well Again.* Los Angeles: Tarcher–St. Martins.

Simonton, O. C., Matthews-Simonton S. (1981). Cancer and stress: counseling the cancer patient. *Med. Journal of Australia.* June 1: 679–683.

Spiegel, D.; Kraemer, H. C.; Bloom, J. R.; Gottheil, E. (1989). The effect of psychosocial treatment on survival of patients with metastatic breast cancer." *Lancet.* October 14, 1989; Vol. II (8668):888–891.

Thomas, C. B., and Duszynski, D. R. Closeness to parents and the family constellation in a prospective study of five disease states: suicide, mental illness, malignant tumor, hypertension, and coronary heart disease. *The Johns Hopkins Medical Journal,* 1973, 134, 251–70.

Recommended Reading

Achterberg, Jeanne: *Imagery in Healing*. Boston: Shambhala, 1985.

Borysenko, Joan: *Minding the Body, Mending the Mind*. New York: Bantam, 1988.

Cousins, Norman: *Anatomy of an Illness*. New York: Norton and Company, Inc. 1979.

Cousins, Norman: *Head First: The Biology of Hope*. New York: Dutton, 1989.

LeShan, L: *Cancer as a Turning Point*. New York: Dutton, 1989.

Maultsby, Maxie C.: *Rational Behavior Therapy*. New Jersey: Prentice Hall, 1984.

Rossi, E.: *The Psychobiology of Mind-Body Healing*. New York: Norton and Company, 1986.

Rossman, Martin L.: *Healing Yourself: A Step-by-Step Program for Better Health Through Imagery*. New York: Walker & Co., 1987.

Siegel, Bernie S.: *Love, Medicine and Miracles*. New York: Harper and Row, 1986.

Simonton, O. Carl, S. Matthews-Simonton and J. Creighton: *Getting Well Again*. New York: Bantam, 1978.

The Simonton Cancer Center

The Simonton Cancer Center provides information, treatment, training and support groups for cancer patients and health care professionals.

The Patient Program is based on the successful model for emotional intervention and support that Dr. Simonton pioneered in the treatment of cancer patients.

It evolved from the concept that beliefs, feelings, attitudes and life-style are important factors affecting health.

When illness occurs, these factors also influence a patient's response to medical treatment and help to determine the effectiveness of the treatment as well as the level of confidence in the medical team.

The program is a five-and-one-half day educational and psychotherapeutic session for cancer patients and their support persons, during which these concepts are explored in a safe, supportive atmosphere conducive to learning and positive change. The program focuses on the influence of beliefs and belief systems. Participants learn techniques for enriching their lives in order to promote their health; lifestyle counseling; and relaxation and mental imagery (creative thinking) exercises. Additionally, participants explore the role of gentleness, and the role of stress, secondary gain, and other contributing factors to disease. The issues of recurrence and death are also examined. By delving into these topics through the use of the group process, patients are enabled to implement these methods in their daily lives.

Our approach is not a replacement for traditional medical treatment. It was originally developed to complement whatever treatment the patients are currently receiving and to maximize their healing potential through their own inner wisdom.

The Simonton Cancer Center also has an intensive internship program for health care professionals and weekend training programs that can be sponsored in your local area.

The Simonton Cancer Center is a non-profit charitable trust and contributions are tax deductible. All contributions go directly to our scholarship fund to assist patients in financial need to attend these programs.

Information on our programs can be obtained by calling or writing:

The Simonton Cancer Center
P.O. Box 890
Pacific Palisades, CA 90272
(310) 459-4434

The Simonton Center Tape and Literature Department
P.O. Box 1198
Azle, TX 76020
(800) 338-2360 or
(817) 444-4073 (in TX)

About the Authors

DR. O. CARL SIMONTON is a radiation oncologist and pioneer in the study of mind-body techniques for treating cancer, documented in the bestselling book *Getting Well Again*, of which he is co-author. He is medical director of the Simonton Cancer Center in Pacific Palisades, California. REID HENSON is an executive with a sizeable U.S. company. He has worked personally with cancer patients for over a decade and lives in Chattanooga, Tennessee. BRENDA HAMPTON is a television writer for Witt/Thomas Productions.